Bakhtin and the
Social Moorings
of Poetry

Bakhtin and the Social Moorings of Poetry

Donald Wesling

Lewisburg
Bucknell University Press
London: Associated University Presses

Associated University Presses
2010 Eastpark Boulevard
Cranbury, NJ 08512

Associated University Presses
Unit 304, The Chandlery
50 Westminster Bridge Road
London SE1 7QY, England

Associated University Presses
P.O. Box 338, Port Credit
Mississauga, Ontario
Canada L5G 4L8

The paper used in this publication meets the requirements of the American National Standard for Permanence of Paper for Printed Library Materials Z39.48-1984.

Library of Congress Cataloging-in-Publication Data

Wesling, Donald.
    Bakhtin and the social moorings of poetry / Donald Wesling.
        p.   cm.
    Includes bibliographical references and index.
    ISBN 0-8387-5540-2 (alk. paper)
    1. Bakhtin, M. M. (Mikhail Mikhailovich), 1895–1975—Contributions in poetics.   2. Poetics.   I. Title.
    PG2947.B3 W47   2003
    808.1—dc21   2003001131

PRINTED IN THE UNITED STATES OF AMERICA

To My Parents
Helene Marguerite Bullinger Wesling
And
Truman Albert Wesling

Contents

Preface

> "[W]e can account for the productivity of language . . . only when we have understood how reference is culturally and historically determined. . . . how the social moorings of language might be understood as essential to it. That is, if we are going to explain how language works, we cannot relegate the social processes of reference to the realm of the 'extralinguistic' as de Man and every other formalist wish to do."
>
> —Satya P. Mohanty, *Literary Theory and the Claims of History* (1997)

OF ALL THE LITERARY TYPES, POETRY IS THE ONE THAT MOST SEEMS TO toss ballast and float free of the dull realism of shore. This is because lyric poetry has come to stand for all poetry, and because lyric poetry has music in its name and makes *cri de coeur* confession its game. Rubbish, of course, but how show this is a mistake? How tie the social moorings of poetry to history and ordinary experience? Mikhail Bakhtin of Russia, the twentieth century's greatest philosopher of communication, had a strong believable answer to this question: the speaking that is in writing is itself necessarily social and historical, and we fight out ideological struggles on the territory of our every utterance. This is a book about how to detach a social reading of poetry from Bakhtin's own reluctance to give it, how to use his terms to produce it, and about what to do once we have it—to answer specific questions about how social speech gets into verse, and to confront the antipoetic prejudice wherever it occurs.

Mikhail Bakhtin (1895–1975) can help us to think about the ways that speaking gets into writing—how we as readers can return utterance, and with it social-historical reference, to novels and plays and poems. After the general introduction, my chapters are on four topics Bakhtin himself considered: dialect, inner speech, rhythm, and the struggle of available languages in an era (called by me the clash of discourses). I explain with examples, usually quoting and closely following whole poems. Most of my examples come from the U.K. and the U.S., with side excursions to Russian guitar poetry of the

9

1970s and to Marina Tsvetaeva in exile from Bolshevik Russia in the early 1920s. With these contents, the book is a modest defense of poetry and poetics against one or two current trends in commentary, with emphasis on practical categories that enable a reading for utterance.

Recently a number of excellent journals have devoted special issues to Bakhtin, and also there is a group of superlative broad-gauge studies of Bakhtin by (for example) Caryl Emerson, Ruth Coates, Alexandar Mihailovich, Ken Hirschkop, and Galin Tihanov. These new articles and books add approaches from many disciplinary directions and are often explicitly in conflict with one another. Their abundance and variety, also their articulate disagreement, are welcome in the special field of Bakhtin studies. One of the few things most of these studies neglect is poetry. My book is in no sense a correction—rather it is a supplement to novel-centered philosophical commentary from the 1970s to 2002.

Bakhtin is notoriously an enemy of (what he considers) the monologism and cry-from-the-heart nature of poetry, in famous statements in the essays chosen by the translators for the anthology, *The Dialogic Imagination* (1981). This reputation obviously must lie athwart the path of my book. I argue first that Bakhtin was not entirely and clearly wrong: there were special logical and special Russian reasons for taking the line he did; and second, that if we are careful to define our terms and our relation to what Bakhtin said, we can apply his most powerful ideas to poetic texts, to find them differently dialogic from the novel, but nonetheless dialogic. So Bakhtin can be followed and extended in contributions to poetics traditionally defined, although he wrote against the great prestige of this ancient field in order to clear a space for the novel.

Chapters 1 and 5 and the several Afterwords, written 2001–2, are intended to frame the special studies of the middle chapters in a more teacher-like language of explanation, and a more political language of social moorings. Chapters 2, 3, and 4 were written for the following International Bakhtin Conferences in the 1990s, at gatherings where novel readers, film students, and philosophers are in a strong majority: Manchester 1991 (my chapter on dialect); Mexico City 1993 (my chapter on inner speech in Basil Bunting); Moscow 1995 (my chapter on rhythm in Marina Tsvetaeva). These three were published as articles, whose titles and other particulars I list below in the Acknowledgments. I have corrected certain minor details in each of these, but have also attached to each an afterword 2002, as a way to address changes in my thinking and in the field, since the time of publication.

A theme of all the chapters is that the notion of dialogism is indispensable to our understanding of poetic writing. I am convinced that by dialogism Bakhtin did not mean cozy conversational back and forth—but rather conflict in language, where speakers try to answer opposing viewpoints in their own statements, where our statements are never entirely our own, as we absorb and also resist influence that comes from outside.

In chapter 1, I offer a polemical rereading of Baktin's thought, from the point of view of poetry, to achieve these purposes: an account of why Bakhtin thought poetry a lesser form than the novel; an account of how a poetics of utterance is a major achievement, if we employ in the dialogic reading of poetry many of the powerful terms Bakhtin invented for the novel; a redefinition of eight of Bakhtin's key terms, from the angle of poetry and poetics; and a proposal supported by many English and American examples, to read with the help of Bakhtin's four most powerful concepts: the speaking subject, clash of inner speech and outer speech, intonation, and the image of a language. In chapter 2, I draw together Bakhtin's many separate references to ideas of dialect and analyze in their social contexts recent poems from Scottish and Caribbean-London writers. In chapter 3, I elaborate Bakhtin's productive idea of inner speech, with relation to the Northumberland modernist poet who died in the mid-1970s: a synthesis of all the works of Basil Bunting from the vantage of this idea and practice. In chapter 4, I argue that when Bakhtin identifies rhythm with meter he is mistaken, and I offer a correction with the help of Henri Meschonnic's great book on rhythm and Richard Cureton's groundbreaking book on rhythmic phrasing. My example is a powerful short-line lyric by Marina Tsvetaeva, quoted in the original Russian and in translation. In chapter 5, I ask how political divisions between schools of recent criticism may help or hinder knowledge of English Romantic writers— our definition and recovery of *their* clashes of discourse after 1789. I find considerable reference to Bakhtin in recent commentary on the Romantic poets, both in passing and in whole books. To bring matters up to yesterday, I end on a clash of discourse between two styles in American poetry in the 1990s.

My thanks to Andrew Wright and Susan Kalter, who helped to

clarify my thinking in the first chapter; and to these groups at UC San Diego: the Humanities Institute, for a Faculty Fellowship in Spring 2002, and the Research Committee of the Academic Senate, for manuscript preparation.

Working with Bakhtin has been a way of keeping my friendly-outsider's relationship to Slavic studies. All thanks to the Slavists, and no blame for my mistakes! My best helpers were teachers of Russian at the University of California, scholars and writers in Russia, the expert on Bakhtin who reviewed this book for the Press, and my wise and scholarly daughter, Molly Wesling.

Acknowledgments

THANKS ARE DUE TO BRIAN ABEL RAGEN, EDITOR, FOR PERMISSION TO RE-print "Mikhail Bakhtin and the Social Poetics of Dialect," from *Papers on Language & Literature* 29,no. 3 (1993): 303–22; and to Ralph Cohen, editor, for permission to reprint four paragraphs and five sentences from "The Speaking Subject in Russian Poetry and Poetics Since 1917," from *New Literary History* 23 (1992): 93–112, used in modified form in chapter 1, and in the afterword to chapter 4. The other two previously published essays in this book come from U.K. journals where the copyright is held by the author of the essay. These are " 'Easier to Die than to Remember': A Bakhtinian Reading of Basil Bunting," from *Durham University Journal,* edited by Richard Caddel (Spring 1995): 83–97; and "Rhythmic Cognition in the Reader: Correcting Bakhtin's Wrong Turn," from *Exploiting Bakhtin,* edited by Alastair Renfrew (Glasgow: University of Strathclyde, 1997): 39–55.

My sincere thanks to the holders of world rights for the passages I have quoted in this book. In the order their materials appear, the copyright holders who have given their permissions are:

Tom Leonard, for permission to quote "Unrelated Incident (3)" and eight lines of "Paroakial," from *Intimate Voices: Selected Work, 1963–1983,* originally published by Galloping Dog Press (Newcastle Upon Tyne, 1983).

Linton Kwesi Johnson, for permission to quote the poem "It dread inna Inglan," from his book *Tings and Times: Selected Poems,* originally published by Bloodaxe Books (Newcastle Upon Tyne, 1991). Copyright Linton Kwesi Johnson, reproduced by kind permission of LKJ Music Publishers Ltd.

Bloodaxe Books for permission to quote passages from Basil Bunting, *Complete Poems* (Highgreen, Tarset, Northumberland: Bloodaxe Books, 2000).

Michael M. Naydan, for permission to quote his translation of Marina Tsvetaeva's first poem in her series "Wires," from this edition:

Marina Tsvetaeva, *After Russia/Posle Rosii*, translated by Michael M. Naydan with Slava Yastremski, annotated by Michael M. Naydan (Ann Arbor: Ardis, 1992).

Bakhtin and the Social Moorings of Poetry

1
The Social Moorings of Poetry

ON THE TERRITORY OF THE UTTERANCE

Purpose and Design

Rᴜssɪᴀɴs sɪᴛ ǫᴜɪᴇᴛʟʏ ᴏɴ ᴛʜᴇɪʀ ʟᴜɢɢᴀɢᴇ ꜰᴏʀ ᴀ ᴍɪɴᴜᴛᴇ ʙᴇꜰᴏʀᴇ ᴛʀᴀᴠ-eling.

The first step on this book's journey is the most difficult to take. If I can succeed in making my point, the other steps will follow. Have I the tact?

If Mikhail Bakhtin is the twentieth century's most profound thinker on human communication, poetry as a form of utterance should be reckoned into his account of speech genres.

That means I need (1) to rescue poetry from Bakhtin's stingy and grumbling description of it; but it also means that I need (2) to use the full range of Bakhtin's communication theory, based on but not limited to a description of the novel, in order to show the clash of inner and outer speech in poems. The second rescue is the more useful and demanding, because a very great deal of commentary on poetry in the past century deliberately neglects the divisions of discourse, the dialogism, that Bakhtin so magnificently shows in ordinary and in literary speech. So I need to criticize Bakhtin in order to use Bakhtin to criticize, and try to make more comprehensive, dominant styles of reading.

This introductory chapter builds the edifice of a poetics of utterance that includes, but works beyond, poetic speech. Bakhtin would approve my decision to focus on *utterance*, which is common to ordinary as to poetic speech. This keeps poetry as not the only or the chief speech genre, rather one among many despite poetry's ancient and exalted, but now diminished, reputation. My design is to show Bakhtin's general views on discourse and person, to re-evaluate his

17

novel-based terminology for the reading of lyric-poetic modes, and to analyze examples with the help of the transcoded terms.

Another design has emerged retrospectively, when I looked at the chapters I had written with a view to making a book. My closely read examples, from the U.K./U.S./former USSR, must to a degree change and adapt the Russian-origin terms through which they are read. An Anglo-American style of reading has become the tint on the Russian lenses.

If that design tends to deterritorialize, my two constitutive metaphors for this book should bring things back to specific placement, because each is a *topos* of topography. The first metaphor for condensing the argument is nautical-spatial: *social moorings of poetry*, by which I mean to convey both separation from and closeness to, as with a ship (the aesthetic) tied up at dock (the social), by many strong lines of attachment. The second metaphor is martial-spatial, Bakhtin's own idea of *fighting out social relationships on the territory of the utterance.* Since this writer's mind is radically perspectival—concerned with placement in space, equally with placement in time—these metaphors for language can keep reminding us of what is central in Bakhtin's thought. These metaphors are reminders of something simple, literal, and universal: *the need of understanding for distance from its object.*

Speaking of distance, on occasion working with Bakhtin involves working beyond Bakhtin: sometimes toward a greater social-liberationist idea of literature in society than his works can plausibly support, and sometimes toward a greater prudence, or skepticism, about social struggles in aesthetic media than either Bakhtin or his Anglo-American liberationist commentators can claim.

"I hear voices in everything"

In 1974, a year before his death, Mikhail Bakhtin wrote some notes on the methodology of the humanities, contrasting his own thought to the depersonalizing, mechanical categories of Structuralism—the critical methodology based on symmetrical oppositions that linguists (like Ferdinand de Saussure) found behind the facts of natural language. Bakhtin objected: "But I hear *voices* in everything and the dialogic relations among them."[1] His work over half a century, that which we have and know he wrote, is a large, intelligent development of this personalistic approach. His antagonists changed from the twenties to the seventies, from Freudianism to Russian Formalism to official Soviet theories of folk art, finally to Structuralism, but the method remained the same: combat theoreticism by *voices*, by insisting on sensitivity to the three-in-one, secular trinity of person-voice-idea, and by developing an ethics or democratics of utterance, of a sort well described in Ken Hirschkop's synoptic book on just this topic.[2] For Bakhtin the word itself contained social struggles. And for us in 2002? In Anglo-American criticism in our time, New Criticism and Deconstruction very often refused to hear voices of the unmechanized and unfinalized human being in literary and other texts, indeed altogether avoided reading for speech acts. So far, too, even the emergent-dominant Postcolonial and Cultural Studies approaches are not consistently dialogic. So a quarter century after his death, what Bakhtin worked through is still a supplement, indeed a completion to current critical modes.

Bakhtin wrote in one of his earliest works on the necessary "non-alibi in Being," by which he meant: No excuses! No apologies![3] Since we need to take personal responsibility for each one of our actions, Bakhtin would not have us say, for instance, "Honor me because I am your parent or spouse, or because I am dying," or "Forgive me because I am asking." That authors should be held to this severe standard, the author of *Bakhtin and the Social Moorings of Poetry* agrees—or will agree after I explain that there is a great deal to do. This book needs to show the pertinence to Anglo-American reading habits of a Russian-speaking, German-influenced, Russian Orthodox thinker who grew up a century ago in Orel, Vilnius, and Odessa, and lived for a long time in provincial Saransk. Bakhtin openly and several times disrespected poetry as an art form. How can his writings be taken against his expressed opinions, as contributions to poetics and the reading of poetry? How can someone who is first and last a philosopher, and who for reasons specific to Russian history turned to novels as examples, be transformed into a teacherly traveler across cultures, disciplines, eras, and modes?

In this book, I select bounded sectors of that explanation. Here in the first chapter, I should like to display and defend the whole coherent circle of Bakhtin's poetics of utterance; and with my profusion of examples, I will develop interconnected definitions to help readers be more speech-conscious and thus be better readers. The overall purpose is to remind readers of poetry that this topic is also Baktin's, that his contribution to poetics, while not definitive, is a major one in his century and consistent with the rest of his theory of communication. Most of what I show is already present though dispersed in Bakhtin and his commentators, so needs to be identified, drawn forth, and linked.

Seven Things I Know about Mikhail Bakhtin

1. He is the most complete theorist of communication acts in the twentieth century; that is, without restricting himself to World, Author, Reader, or Work, he can move among the several orientations.
2. More persuasively than any other twentieth-century thinker, he is able to explain the working of alterity as the defining condition governing the perception of selves (we can never see the self as finished—we can only see others that way), and the perception of whole societies. With Bakhtin we absolutely leave behind the Cartesian philosophical subject, because the other helps to constitute the self, in endless dialogue.
3. Bakhtin's persistent habit of reading for utterances and not for any other linguistic unit, forces the pertinent suppressed question of much literary analysis, the first and most philosophical of literary questions: Who is speaking? Add, as he always does, Who is the addressee?, and we have the two most productive of all literary questions.
4. Ideas, utterances, are always the same kinds of entities, and always located in the person in Mikhail Bakhtin; he has not accepted, though he knows, the modern and postmodern idea that a voice may be separated from a personality. For him, there is no such thing as textual voice.
5. There is in Bakhtin a tight fit between his ethics and his aesthetics and linguistics of the utterance: he tends to assimilate art-language to ordinary speech, though he at all times shows he knows the difference. It works equally in the other direction, so that the author is for him one of the strongest images of a morally aware construction of a self.
6. While Bakhtin and members of his school—Valentin Voloshinov, Pavel Medvedev—focus on the unique speech event, this does not imply a radical subjectivism. They insist on the social moorings of the utterance, its saturation with ideological meaning.

7. Bakhtin's estimation of the novel at the expense of poetry can be understood, forgiven, and overridden if (with caution) we use his dialogic terms for poetry as well as for prose. If we can correct his wrong turn on poetic rhythm, we can develop a dialogics of lyric and a more positive, or at least more historically situated, valuation of epic.

Mikhail Bakhtin and Poetry

Nearly always, when Bakhtin wrote of poetry he compared it to narrative prose and found it lacking. He was unable to see behind this opposition, despite the fact that elsewhere his work is immensely sophisticated in eluding other easy oppositions between self and other, self and society, literary and nonliterary, spoken and written, space and time. Rhetorically and polemically he needed to pull poetry down from its royal position at the head of the hierarchy of types, in order to bring narrative prose up from the bottom.

Russian poetics generally, up to and including Formalism in the twenties (but with exceptions such as Viktor Shklovsky's account of the novel's versatility), had drawn a sharp line between poetic language in its controlled and formal cosmos, and prose language in its aleatory or chaotic abandon. As if prose were not also carefully structured but by different principles than meter and the line, as if prose could not itself be monologic for certain effects! Bakhtin did more than just reverse a prejudice, though admittedly his bravado performance contained some dazzling condemnatory phrases against poetry's asocial qualities, and against a poetics and linguistics that justified earlier claims for the kingship of poetry.

The poetry-over-prose prejudice was a notably Russian one that still haunts the minds of critics and writers on that territory, because it is rooted in the Russian Orthodox trust in the Word: kerygma, the incarnate god in language. As Steven Cassedy has shown, from Roman Jakobson to many post-Soviet critics and poeticians, including many not subscribing to Orthodox tenets, this trust in the Word had a literary corollary: the Word is best embodied in the vanquished difficulty of poetry and not in realistic daily prose, so there must be a rigorous and essential distinction between types.[4]

For Bakhtin, in his polemical response to this prejudice, the basic position was that poetry was asocial because it was monologic, single-voiced, suppressing half of a dialogue; that in particular, lyric poetry was non-narrative, less able therefore to bring in a thick reference to social fact, the conflict of languages and perspectives in historical social life; and finally, as one result of traditional rules, as well as of single-voicing, poetic rhythm regularized sound and sense in the utterance, so that what was self-centered was also paradoxically turned into a strict procrustean bed of convention.

This was the argument, and with it Bakhtin was able to mount a coherent and successful defense of the novel as a modern form. He did not need the opposition to poetry except as a starting point, because his philosophy of acts of communication—his poetics of the utterance—buoyed up his theory and history of the novel, and taken in context his account of the novel is an instance of a philosophy of responsible human agency. So I shall argue that the prose-poetry opposition is not only refutable (this has been done elsewhere by others, and at some length in this book), but also a historical construction that we cannot permit to block our work.

Before we get on with our work, though, it is only fair to concede that Bakhtin's attack is cogent in its widest phrasing, when he takes poetry as poeticization, idealism as such. The mythos of poetry as a singular or sacred language, suppressing conflicts in its own history and suppressing the presence of other-languagedness, deserves Bakhtin's scorn—and ours. I might mention, too, that Bakhtin himself was able to think beyond the opposition, when necessary: he twice analyzed the clash of discourses in Pushkin's poem, "Parting," in essays of the 1920s; his account of Goethe as poet, in essays of the 1930s, is as full of admiration and insight as his account of Goethe as novelist; and the archival reel-to-reel tape of Bakhtin in the 1970s reciting German, Russian, and French poems, played at the Moscow Bakhtin Conference in 1995, showed perfect memory and subtle intonation.

Below, I would like to transcode some of Bakhtin's key terms, redefining them for poetry and poetics; these are too productive and interesting to be reserved for the novel. All poems should be open to dialogic reading by the use of habits derived from these terms, not just those narrative types of poems Bakhtin might have called "novelized." In fact, the main claim is that previous Anglo-American scholarship has drastically underestimated the role of speaking in writing, and recourse to Bakhtin's categories will return to us a whole, nearly lost dimension of poetic art.[5]

On the Territory of the Utterance

In the middle of a brilliantly repetitive, poetry attacking, 150 paged essay of 1934–35, "Discourse in the Novel," Bakhtin writes this difficult paragraph containing typical phrases on art-speech as conflict:

> While noting the individual element in intentional hybrids, we must once again strongly emphasize the fact that in novelistic artistic hybrids that structure *the image of a language,* the individual element, indispensable as it is for the actualization of language and for its subordination to the artistic whole of the novel (here the destinies of languages are interwoven with the individual destinies of speaking persons), is nevertheless inexorably merged with the socio-linguistic element. In other words, the novelistic hybrid is not only double-voiced and double-accented (as in rhetoric) but is also double-languaged; for in it there are not only (and not even so much) two individual consciousnesses, two voices, two accents, as there are two socio-linguistic consciousnesses, two epochs, that, true, are not here unconsciously mixed (as in an organic hybrid), but that come together and consciously fight it out on the territory of the utterance.[6]

There is here some unnecessary awkwardness, and not only in the obscurity of syntax and of several parentheses and concessions; also certain terms, like "intentional," "artistic hybrid," "image of a language," "double-voiced," and "double-accented," are off-putting in the absence of the context of Bakhtin's preceding argument. What makes the paragraph, indeed the whole baggy essay, worth our attention is Bakhtin's habit of finding useful new distinctions and memorable metaphors in the process of elaborating his version of dialogism—which is more richly social than just dialogue, or conversation.

"The image of a language," an opaque notion neglected by Bakhtin's commentators, is so important to poetry and poetics that in this chapter I devote a section to it. Briefly here, it may be defined as a special language or limited register, a language-within-language as represented in a work of verbal art. It could be an actual or possible language, stylized, or even, if we suppose beyond Bakhtin, an impossible language, as projected or imagined in the future or among nonhumans—animals or aliens.

In explaining a poetics of utterance, the most helpful points to draw from the paragraph are:

1. utterances are not only spoken; utterances are also the orality or the spoken within the written, and notably within art-writing;
2. utterances may appear unitary, but each of them is riven into "two consciousnesses, two language-intentions, two *voices*" in Bakhtin's words from a nearby sentence;
3. utterances are divided by analysis not only into two agonistic consciousnesses, needing to be defined separately and together, but also may be read for the social and historical contradictions within/behind the apparently unified voice of the text; and
4. Since two epochs "fight it out on the territory of the utterance," the language of artistic works (including, we now say, poems) is always imbricated in historical struggle, even when not obviously so. Every utterance is a smaller or larger war despite a sound-look that presents it as pacified, at one.

These are the meanings compressed into the title of this chapter.

When I tell my three-year-old grandson, as I put on his sneakers, "You're going to play with Kylie and Shannon at the beach; girls are fun to play with," I am telling him what will happen and adding an editorial comment, both to cheer him up and to discourage the signs of a male-superior attitude he is learning from television cartoons. As hearer of a face-to-face utterance with two language-intentions, from a speaker, me, from another era, he does not reply verbally, but one response will be how he plays with the girls at the water's edge. Structurally the same but at a higher level of generality is Keats's method of organizing "Ode to a Nightingale" with an admirable but consciously antiquated language of fantasy ("O, for a draught of vintage!"), set against an equally admirable language of brutal realism ("Here, where men sit and hear each other groan"): each system of metaphors representing a different and opposed historical era, or, as Bakhtin shows in the final chapter of his book on Rabelais, the way we see a novelist mocking the unitary language of medieval scholasticism, with the multiple vernaculars of a new era, as yet un-named.

The phrase, both martial and geographical, about fighting it out on the territory of the utterance, will now summarize a coherent account of human language and literature; and my own three rudimentary instances may stand for more, to explain Bakhtin's most basic assumption, along a linked chain of premises. Thus, literature represents a conflict; and this because the language out of which it is made represents a conflict; and this because reality itself is alterity at every level, a non-coincidence of minds, selves, outer and inner speech acts, perspectives, social classes, and historical eras. In time, because of hope and habit, which dissolved context, what is riven comes to appear sutured, and a divided utterance begins to form a covering fabric of uniformity—whose name may be either person, meaning writerly or signature style, or historical era, meaning period style. One of the first tasks for a reader or philosophical critic, in this tradition, will be to comb apart into several and conflicted languages what has come to sound settled, single.

Of course, some readers may be incompetent, or may lack knowledge or stamina, or may be unsympathetic to the genre, or may read to confirm a prejudice. The most fully dialogic readers are, however, likely to be attentive to whole works, generous in acceptance of creative thinking, resourceful in resistance to the text's claims.

The more we know about an utterance, the more we find emerging a linguistic and social struggle whose combatants or discussants we are identifying. If the utterance is literary—in the restricted usage of this book, meaning *represented speech within writing*—we get a successful impression of a contained unity, along with the counter-impression of a social struggle still engaged, or being overcome. Marxist social critics such as V. N. Voloshinov and Pavel Medvedev, friends with whom Bakhtin collaborates in the twenties, and others since, are keen to see the social struggle brought into the open. For them, any restriction to a sole line of critical inquiry into the contained unity of a single style is Formalism, always a mistake. However, Formalism in such figures as Viktor Shklovsky and Yurii Tynianov, for all its errors, never committed the capital error of Voloshinov and Medvedev, which was partly to discredit, or perhaps just neglect, the contained unity of literary style where several voices tend to get resolved into the one voice of the text. Bakhtin himself, unpinnable as either Marxist or Formalist, usually keeps more flexibly aware than his friends, of the rifts within the unities and of the singularity of style in its process of resolving divisions.

The Buds of Future Form and Content

Very likely V. N. Voloshinov wrote "Discourse in Life and Discourse in Poetry: Questions of Sociological Poetics" [Slovo v zhizni i slovo v poezii], and, if he did, he was certainly so closely in tune with Bakhtin that this is a crucial essay in any plan to pull together a Bakhtinian poetics of utterance.[7] The essay, attributed to Voloshinov in the translated volume *Bakhtin School Papers* (1983) and with an authorship never disputed by Bakhtin himself or serious work in the field, contains even as early as the mid twenties many elements of the developed communication theory. In the title, Russian *slovo* is correctly translated as "discourse," but it may also be translated as "word," for the Russian comprehends these two ideas while English is restricted to one. Sometimes the title is mistranslated "Discourse in Life and Discourse in Art," an error which reinforces Western Bakhtin scholarship's bias against poetry, although the essay itself speaks about poetry when it touches matters literary.

The speaker of this essay describes himself as a "Marxist sociologist," whose mission is to correct all Formalist ideas of "the immanent . . . analysis of literature and its autonomous laws" (6), as well as any fetishism of the literary device, any reading from "an abstract linguistic point of view" (8). Against these theoreticist errors, Voloshinov sets a poetics of social interaction, of "cocreative perception" (9), and above all a need to test art-speech against its "foundations" in "ordinary *real-life speech*" (10). Such testing occurs, for example, in *intonation*—"on the border of the verbal and the nonverbal" (14)—where we read context to complete the meaning of an utterance. "Intonation establishes," Voloshinov says, "an intimate connection between discourse and the non-verbal context. Living intonation . . . leads discourse beyond its verbal limits" (13). Intonation is usually neglected in traditional poetic analysis, but for Voloshinov and Bakhtin it is a crucial diagnostic feature because it is social and broadens out into space and time; so I return to this category below, as one of four crucial terms.

"Living intonation" derives from the energies of speech in the concrete utterance, from social meanings as sounded, and thus it has life before linguistic abstractions ensue. Voloshinov in this essay is very like Bakhtin in his habit of deriving art-speech from ordinary speaking. He uses an example, one that has made this essay memorable, where a silent couple sits in a room and one says "Well!"

(tak!), just as both glance out the window, "both sick of the pro-
tracted winter" (11) as they see it is snowing in the month of May.
The one word carries, through intonation, the whole implied context: the meaning of "the utterance depends upon the participants'
real, material participation in one and the same section of being"
(11), says Voloshinov, who goes on to find in this "Well!" a source
and allegory of literary form. He discovers in the "real-life utterance" something he calls "*artistic potentials, the buds of future form and
content*" (17), deriving art from, and assimilating art to, speech. Inci-
dentally, this is very like what Bakhtin argues in all his writings, and
is expressed in a biological metaphor (buds) that is a characteristic
defining gesture for Bakhtin himself. Late in his career, in the individual essays translated in the English-language anthology *Speech
Genres*, Bakhtin would develop the same idea, with his distinction between the primary speech genres of real-life utterance, and the secondary speech genres of literature, which regularize, and distort,
speech into style. For Bakhtin, novels are closer to real-life utterance
than poems. However, from the point of view of my book in 2002,
once we have made the move into secondary speech genres, the degree of speech-ness is immaterial. Critics explicitly influenced by
Bakhtin, since the 1960s, take the view that the main issue is: real-
life utterance or represented real-life utterance? Plainly both novels
and poems are on the secondary side of the line.[8]

For our purposes, the most promising sociological account of this
cluster of issues is by Dana Polan, who writes: "Far from traditional
aesthetic notions of poetry as the elevated complexification of refer-
ential discourse, Bakhtin deconstructs the standard values of the
poetry/prose distinction by finding in the obsessive singularity of
the poetic word a monologic reduction of the semantic richness of
the dialogue of everyday language. Emphatically, however, this is a
deconstruction and not a simple reversal on Bakhtin's part, since his
notion of a dialogism underlying all speech-acts—even ones that
seek to repress the dialogical imagination—leads back to a new reading of poetry: a reading of the ways in which it reveals sites of dialogism between the crevices of a dominant monologism."[9] I am not
convinced that Bakhtin intended this to be a deconstruction of the
poetry/prose distinction, but it seems to me that Polan does point
the way for a stronger Bakhtin-influenced criticism of poetry, and in
general a workable poetics for the next century: the key proposal
and watchword is for "a reading of the ways in which [poetry] re-

veals sites of dialogism between the crevices of a dominant monologism." To offer a quick comparison: the tepid, unenergetic free verse
of *The New Yorker*, lost in its surround of advertisements, lacks an
edge to pull on or cut with, indeed speaks to and for the social domi-
nants of our moment. By contrast certain small press chapbooks,
some of surpassing difficulty, slow down the reader's reception,
force a struggle for meaning through ugliness, or sound-distortion,
or thematizing writing within writing, or denying speech and narrative and thus marking them as precious. By many other means these
latter find the sites of dialogism, of some kind of resistance, even if
not making direct political statements. But whatever their politics,
statemental political poems like Muriel Rukeyser's multi-part docu-
mentary, *The Book of the Dead* (1938), are also more dialogic than
what the glossies bring to their huge publics.

What is the most democratic form of dialogism in writing? What
form of authorial utterance increases the freedom of the reader?
What kinds of experiences increase the odds that we might train
readers both generous and resistant? For a writer of any era to make
evident through obliquities of writing that there may be heteroglossia and double-voicing—many languages within English, thus multiple social sites, not one—is ultimately more democratic a gesture
than boldly to contradict the dominant monologism. However, direct denunciation also has its uses. Despite Bakhtin's opinion in this
matter, nearly everywhere in the epoch of modernity a multi-lan-
guaged poetry has widened the crevices by expanding sites of dialogism. In just this sense, and often employing the complexity Dana
Polan says Bakhtin deplores, poetry criticizes and recruits language.[10]

*Two socio-linguistic consciousnesses, two epochs . . . that come together
and consciously fight it out on the territory of the utterance:* in the closely
read examples in chapters 2–5 below, these conscious struggles
occur within the writing, whose implicit poetics is also a politics.
Scottish and Caribbean-London dialect writers and Basil Bunting
the Northumberland patriot (chapters 2 and 3) stand against dominant English places, persons, and languages. Marina Tsvetaeva writing from exile (chapter 4) finds new homes after she is expelled
from an utterly transformed Bolshevik Russia; and finds a love connection outside marriage with an idealized Boris Pasternak, a
rhythm beyond meter, Russian language outside Russia. Recent
commentators on Romanticism try to explain how two epochs may

be coordinated, and from their rhetoric it may seem the earlier era, after 1789, is the screen on which our own 1970s-90s ideological struggles are fought out (chapter 5). Not one of the writers and theorists I take up in the body of this book is only a personal speaker or an isolated consciousness.

In the preface, I indicated that this first chapter and the last chapter are both more teacher-like and more explicitly political than the middle chapters. Here at the end of the first part of the first chapter, before I cross the seam between the political (what's above) and the pedagogical (to follow to chapter's end), I should explain my position on social readings of poems. I cannot write with the certainties of my colleagues and friends in the field, or of my former self when I produced in the 1970s a Marxist reading of Keats's "Ode to a Nightingale" as an ambiguous expression of class unrest in the year 1819.[11] I am aware that my constitutive metaphor of social moorings will put poetry closely next to society, but not in the center of it, and that it rouses expectations of an inside-outside opposition that it should be our task to abolish. I am as worried as left Bakhtinians, such as David Shepherd, that drawing out from Bakhtin one more technology of reading to add to the list of methods we have will not give a poetics of social forms. Shepherd's contention is that "in such a situation the most immediately useful aspect of Bakhtin is precisely that close attention to features of texts which has so often led to his being used in a markedly conservative way."[12] Since I am about to deliver pages that encourage close attention through both categories and examples, here are my reasons for going forward.

Mikhail Bakhtin's philosophy of communication has been appropriated by many methodologies as a good fit with their own way of thinking—including methods in logical contradiction, and in political opposition. Sometimes Bakhtin seems, indeed, in contradiction with himself on certain topics. There has never been an adequate Marxist account of Bakhtin's social theories that explains the reservations and contradictions, and Galin Tihanov's recent book shows how Bakhtin's account of the novel contrasts with that of a determined Marxist, Georg Lukács.[13] It would be possible to set up a more systematic and certain social reading, by specifying Bakhtin's contradictions and laying out one's own divergences from his complex position, but the energy expended in nuance of counterarguing would take up the first half of one's study: and would the result be in any strong sense a Bakhtinian theory?

Instead, in the present book my plan will be to present dialogue and utterance in verbal art as already social, and to define in what way those speech acts may be specified by class, gender, nation, and historical conditions of possibility. This is absolutely in the spirit of Bakhtin and adheres to his core positions in philosophy. The advantage of this is that the categories for emphasis—speaking subject, clash of inner and outer speech, intonation, image of a language— are not formalist categories but, as types of speaking within writing, define a range of social relationships, usually more collective than individual. Whatever is methodological and pedagogical in the ensuing pages is therefore also political.

Social Moorings, as title metaphor implying difference and distance, seems to reinstate the inside-outside or text-context dilemma. But this is immediately mitigated by the continuous act of mooring, where the lines extend into both entities, and the lines bind together and act as channels of communication both ways. By inference, moorings are dialogues.

Recognizing that "it is far from easy to know exactly where or how to begin to use a Bakhtinian theory of reading" (151), David Shepherd has a positive program, too. His phrasing is one I accept as my own: "Bakhtinian textual analysis, if predicated on a proper, thorough understanding of dialogism and the utterance, offers possibilities of working 'from the inside out' in such a way that the very difficulties of 'active understanding' can become a means of making explicit the conditions of possibility of that understanding and of past understandings of the text" (151). My final chapter is my best approach to such a broad-gauge method of reading, but to my mind a thorough understanding of dialogism and the utterance is to be built up by many smaller kinds of attentions, such as those I describe next.

READING WITH AND BEYOND BAKHTIN:
DEFINITIONS AND EXAMPLES FOR A POETICS OF UTTERANCE

Re-Evaluating for Poetry the Terms of Bakhtin's Philosophy

Half a century of productive thinking, from the 1920s to the 1970s, takes a writer through changes of topic, antagonist, method. With the care of historians of ideas, Bakhtin's recent synoptic commentators have mapped Bakhtin's intellectual commitments, from Neo-Kantian, to Russian Orthodox lay theologian, to apparent and then dissenting Marxist, and so on. Nonetheless, certain indispensable ideas re-occur from era to era in his marches on the territory of the utterance, gaining new meanings from change of context: rather continuous embroidery than frequent abrupt instances of about-face.

Some translations and volumes of commentary, for instance the Michael Holquist translation of *The Dialogic Imagination* (1981) and the first edition of *Bakhtin and Cultural Studies,* essays edited by Ken Hirschkop and David Shepherd (1989), contain glossaries of key terms in Bakhtin's vocabulary.[14] There seems to be a consensus in Bakhtin studies that we still require a huge philosophical thesaurus of interrelated synonyms, to account for the systematic nature—or what can be reckoned so—of Bakhtin's thought. One accepts the difficulties of this synthesizing impulse, in order to show the coherence and usefulness of unit-ideas. There is plainly a risk of conflating periods in his thought, overriding changes and contradictions. There is also the risk of importing interpretations from the commentator, somewhat reduced here by the abundance of examples: I offer examples for nearly every category, but working with quick ostensive gestures must mean that no item can be treated with fullness of analysis. What follows is a practical prelude to future, more adequate reading in Bakhtin's spirit, with his terms.

Here, with a view to influencing skillful readers by making them more conscious of what they already know, I will give an elaborated glossary, first and quickly for six oppositions and eighteen terms from Mikhail Bakhtin's general communication theory, then at greater length with the four terms I consider most productive for poetry and poetics. To situate all three of these arrays in terms of Bakhtin's thought, I will offer a summary, admittedly nonhistorical and partial, of Bakhtin's positions as a philosophical critic.[15]

If there is one idea that can be used to open out Bakhtin's thought, that idea is *alterity.* For Bakhtin, we can never know ourselves or see ourselves as finished beings, so we require the otherness of other people to define us in the world (as we reciprocally define other people by seeing them from the outside). Alterity is the defining condition governing the perception of persons, but also defining the perception of whole societies. Bakhtin is the philosopher of nonharmonious wholes, of shared differences.

That is why his thought is built of terms that we latecomers may set out in dyads, as terms for simultaneously interacting differences, which can be listed here with the preferred terms first. One must remember that the terms are always in rapport, or in struggle, not one without the other, moored across a gap.

CENTRIFUGAL/CENTRIPETAL: Cultural and artistic trends, in eras of expansion or contraction.

CARNIVAL REVERSAL/OFFICIAL CULTURE: Terms from the Rabelais book for tendencies toward resistance or acceptance, in the culture of an era.

HETEROGLOSSIA/MONOGLOSSIA: In a given era, do speech genres let dialects and points of view multiply, or not?

INTERNALLY PERSUASIVE SPEECH/OFFICIAL OR AUTHORITATIVE SPEECH: Terms for the struggle for authentic utterance, within the discourse of an era or a single text.

NOVEL/POETRY: The novel is multi-voiced, polyphonic, whereas poetry is monologic, restricted to merely personal speech and opinion.

DIALOGIC/MONOLOGIC: The dialogic allows the otherness of the other, and requires alterity; the monologic is only one voice speaking to itself, or turning the other into the self.

The final dyad is the most general, and the most powerful as a tool for thinking. Bakhtin rejects the philosophy of possessive individualism, where the self (since Descartes) is enclosed in a shell of personhood and consciousness, develops independently. For him, the only way to understand the self is in relation to the addressee; there is no sealed-off, bounded, singular self, no autotelic utterance. In fact, utterance is a variable unit of analysis, and utterances of many types are what we study as literary-social facts. Utterances comprise what one person says, adjusting to the other's state of apprehension, and what another says in reply; the system of utterances and responses will contain the interruptions, and the very volatile beginnings and endings of speeches, where dialogic partners seem to overlap. The utterance can be as small as a one word speech in ordinary conversation or in art, or as large as the three volume set, in eighteen hundred pages, of *The History of the Decline and Fall of the Roman Empire.*

There is a developmental dimension in the philosophy of utterance, which is hinted at times in Bakhtin but better explained by his contemporary, psychologist Lev Vygotsky (who died in 1934). As children we move into a world of already-existing utterances; at first, we are necessarily colonized by outer speech—that is how we learn to speak. However, as we develop as persons, increasingly we fend off some words, and wrest into ownership the words we want and need. Moral freedom is owning one's own utterances, and the most basic unit of mature democratic culture is an exchange: the open giving and receiving of public speech.[16]

Of course, in our messy engagement in actual public discourse, our utterances, and utterances in our works of verbal art, are never free or easy. Utterance is always, but never entirely, subject to determining constraints; and the naming and (if needed) overcoming of those constraints is in our era a central type of literary-cultural criticism. Bakhtin was not the first to insist that readers identify social tones produced by struggles on the territory of the utterance, but his account was the most fully argued and philosophically rich. To go beyond his work is to offer warrants for the claim: if such struggles are present in, and indeed organize, novels they are bound to do the same in poems. However, one exceeds him, in this, first by developing for poetry the very set of terms that he defined and defended.

Transcoding for Poetry the Definitions of Bakhtin's Critical Terms

These terms deserve more space to elaborate the definitions and examples, because of the complexity of the issues involved in moving from Russian to English and from prose to poetry. Claiming these terms for poetry is in itself contentious. To argue each of these fully to the bottom would take up too much of the chapter, but to drop the terms would diminish the picture I need to show of the wide reach and usefulness of Bakhtin's habitual counters of thought. I have elected to display the range, to center it around examples mostly from my own special studies below in the book, and to find what value I can in brevity and suggestiveness.

CENTRIFUGAL: A vector of changing forces in language and culture, from the poem to its larger social context, widening outward. (Example: the appeal to Thatcher era U.K. history in chapter 2 below.)

CENTRIPETAL: A vector of changing forces in language and culture, from the larger social context to the poem, narrowing inward. (Example: the appeal to poems by Wordsworth and Opie, as exam-

ples of antislavery discourse in the Romantic era, in chapter 5
below.)

CARNIVAL REVERSAL: Changes of speaker, stance, and tone in a
poem—from dignified elevation to scatology, or to working-class
perspective. (Example: the violent cruel final image in Randal Jar-
rell's short poem, "The Death of the Ball Turret Gunner.")

HETEROGLOSSIA: Multi-languagedness in poetry: shifts of registers
within standard language, or shifts from standard to dialect. (Example: dialect speech in Tom Leonard and Linton Kwesi Johnson in
chapter 2 below.)

MONOGLOSSIA: single-languagedness in poetry: the presumed lyric
cry, or the poetry of statemental assertion. (Example: Keats's direct
appeal to the reader in his short lyric, "This Living Hand.")

INTERNALLY PERSUASIVE DISCOURSE: When the speaker of a poem
claims to own his or her own experience, and there is a good likeli-
hood the claim is correct. (Example: the love-testimony sections of
Basil Bunting's long poem, *Briggflatts.*)

AUTHORITATIVE DISCOURSE: Opposite of *Internally Persuasive.* This
term, in Bakhtin, can mean top-down and monologic, as the discourse of those in power. (Example: the discourse of newspapers, as
mocked in the political section of Bunting's *Briggflatts.*) But the
term does not have a uniformly negative cast, and can also mean the
voice of a loving parent, or of God.

NOVEL: The storytelling territory of utterances-in-struggle, double-
voicing, and polyphony; poetry occupies most of the same territory,
but with fewer utterers and utterances, and often with a less elaborated narrative structure. (Example: George Eliot's *Middlemarch.*)

POETRY: The lyricized territory of utterances-in-struggle, double-
voicing, and polyphony, "genres that are poetic in the narrow
sense," no less than the novel a heteroglot genre. This definition
stands against Bakhtin's frequent and reasoned dismissal of poetic
utterance as monologic, but finds some support in Bakhtin himself,
who in the early work *Art and Answerability* wrote: "Language reveals
all its possibilities only in poetry."[17]

DIALOGIC: The adjective form of Bakhtin's key term. When utterer and utterance take account of the possible reply of an addressee; once there are *at least two* in the world of discourse, there
may be many more speakers. From the noun *DIALOGISM*, which
means not or not merely conversational talk, but rather a philosoph-
ical-political mode of agency. Michael Holquist in his book *Dialogism*

speaks of the dialogic mode of agency as "a version of relativity," and as the primary instance of differences that cannot and should not be overcome.[18] (Example: Elizabeth Barrett Browning's speech to Robert Browning in her *Sonnets From the Portugese*.)

MONOLOGIC: When an utterer and utterance do not take account of the possible reply of an addressee; the discourse of power, in ordinary language or art language. (Example: radio talk show hosts who permit only call-in comments from persons who share the host's politics.)

CANONIZATION: "The tendency in every form to harden its generic skeleton and elevate the existing norms to a model that resists change."[19] Bakhtin felt the novel has no canon while poetry is preeminently the canonical form, but these tendencies appear to operate in history regardless of generic assignment or degree of heteroglossia. (Examples: the cult of Shakespeare across all of Europe in the nineteenth century, well described in a recent book by Péter Dávidházi, and G. B. Shaw's sense of daring when he mocked Shakespeare at century's end.)

CHRONOTOPE: "Time-Space": "An optic for reading texts as x-rays of the forces at work in the culture system from which they spring."[20]

IDEOLOGEME: "Every speaker . . . is an ideologue and every utterance an Ideologeme,"[21] and this regardless of speech genre. (Examples: principled revolt against standard English in the dialect poets described in chapter 2; Tsvetaeva's resistant-nostalgic exile's relationship to Russia, described in the account of her poem "Wires" in chapter 4 below.)

REFRACTION: Author's angle of entry into the many separate utterances of a work, on the analogue of bending of light rays. The poetic persona may be similar to the biographical experience of the poetic author, but never entirely overlaps, so poetic voices refract too, like the novel but perhaps at a shallower angle. (Example: greater claim to bardic roles and to personal insertion in the poems of William Butler Yeats, by comparison to the disappearance of T. S. Eliot as a person, especially from Eliot's early poems.)

VOICE: "Speaking consciousness;"[22] voice is a metaphor of the subject whether in prose or poetry. Not only prose is dialogic and double-voiced, just as not only poetry is monologic and single-voiced. (Examples brief and extended are in every chapter below, whenever passages from poems are quoted and commented upon.)

SPEECH GENRE: A category of writing, defined according to dominant speech acts the writing contains. This is not an oxymoron, but a category that defines art speech by a modifier from natural language, so as to show the co-presence of both within the formal utterance. (Examples: the gestures traditionally made in prefaces and introductions and footnotes; the essay as a form; the dramatic monologue; the poems of personal address to a named addressee.)

ZONES: There are for Bakhtin character zones and speech zones, which must always be occupied by recognizable persons, that is, moral agents whether fictional or actual. These are places of "autonomous voice," but this phrase need not always mean places locatable in biographical selves. Bakhtin is sophisticated enough to see that, in Michael Davidson's term, "propositions of 'subject'" may stand in for biographical selves.[23]

Beyond Bakhtin, we now see that there may be characters in poems (such as Victorian dramatic monologues like Tennyson's "Ulysses") as well as in novels, and that there do exist in modern and postmodern works zones of character and speech that belong to no one: textual voice, unimaginable by Bakhtin but certainly created in novels and in poems of the twentieth century.

Examples of Bakhtinian zones of speech may be found in the way first-person literary narrators, tellers of short tales in poetry, quote or pretend to quote others, selecting a version of the discourse of others: Tatiana's language in Pushkin's *Eugene Onegin* is Bakhtin's own example; also there is Tom Leonard's Glasgow-Scots poem in chapter 2, and the actual invented dialogues, speech within speech, quoted in recent Scottish monologue-novels like Alasdair Gray's *Janine 1982* and Irvine Welsh's *The Marabou Stork Nightmares.*

The Four Most Productive Terms, Defined and with Examples

Chapter 3 below is organized around *inner speech.* I pursue this term further here, by new synthetic descriptions and several more examples, and I put the term more into tension with a dialogic partner, *outer speech.* Also I now bring three further Bakhtinian categories as reminders for critical readers: *speaking subject, intonation,* and *the image of a language.* These other three terms look more obviously social, but of course all Bakhtin's synonyms for utterance are entirely social and historical.

I intend a selection of brief analyses to demonstrate the usefulness of each of the four productive terms, taking instances from a standard anthology of English and American poetry. Ubiquity of example, along with reproducibility of analysis, are what I intend; so I need only suggest typical ways a term can focus attention. The examples are all well known to the general reader—but not, or perhaps not fully consciously, these ways of interpreting on the territory of the poetic utterance.

The Speaking Subject

The older linguistics, before Bakhtin and also after but not influenced by him, relied on the older idea of the philosophical subject as an isolated mind, neither taking nor giving influence. The older linguistic subject, as a source of language units, was separated from others for the more convenient study of units of language from phoneme to sentence. Rarely did these units push above the sentence into what linguists used to call *suprasegmentals,* so for them a discourse-linguistics was impossible. When discourse linguistics did come in, during the 1960s in the work of Teun A. Van Dijk and others, it was still based upon the old, Kantian-Hegelian idea of a philosophical subject—a self-possessing individual with a life history, personhood, and free will.

The idea of a speaking (*not* a philosophical) subject, which Bakhtin shares with others in the twentieth century, notably French workers in poetics such as Julia Kristeva and Henri Meschonnic, is a narrowing of the possible range to the territory only of the utterance: the self as it can be spoken, and always interacting with an addressee whether present or absent. The Russian is *govoriashchii ia,* the speaking I or the speaking person, and Bakhtin employs the term several times in his thirties piece "Discourse in the Novel"— also in the fifties–seventies essays his English-speaking interpreters have collected for the book they called *Speech Genres.* Bakhtin never defines the term, except massively in context in his account of person in relation to utterance, so it is up to his commentators to draw forth a description of his intent. This self that is speaking puts a premium on what can be uttered to an addressee and, in the Bakhtin Circle, excludes what cannot be uttered; notably it omits the unconscious, and de-emphasizes, or as in the Rabelais book, collectivizes what is visceral in emotion-speech. Bakhtin calls this a trans-linguistics, because it refuses to divide discourse by units below, at, and above the sentence, and rather takes the living utterance as the unit.

To phrase the same thing another way, this kind of study puts utterance between two consciousnesses, on the borderline between speaker and addressee, and influential in both directions.

So the narrowing is also a powerful reimagining of communication theory, because it makes every utterance the territory of social interaction. Caryl Emerson has helpfully explained Bakhtin's utterance as an *energy* that *negotiates* between person and person, premised on the inevitable distance between persons: the spatial metaphor of a "situation" where the orientation of a voice "is measured by the field of responses it evokes," and where, Emerson says, "every speaking subject speaks something of a foreign language to everyone else" and thus performs and calls forth acts of translation.[24] And that work on the leading edges of two consciousnesses *is* speaking: the "verbal negotiability of each person or utterance vis-à-vis every other," and a resultant aesthetics of self-abnegation.[25] That is, for a philosophy that admits the other into the origins of discourse, a willingness to surrender something, to have permeable outlines, is part of normal struggle on the territory of the utterance.

Wlad Godzich, arguing that "Bakhtin identified *discourses* as vectors of cultural conflicts," goes further than Emerson to emphasize the agonistic nature of the dialogic principle. Godzich argues that Bakhtin and his circle actually anticipated that "the central conflict in this postmodern society [Russia and the world after the break in 1989] would be a *cultural* one" where a generalized field of conflicting discourses "slices through individuals."[26] There is much in Bakhtin's own writing to give warrant for Godzich's postmodern formulation, that "Discourses are carriers of cultural orientations, and they have the capacity to endow with subject position those who wield them." However, Bakhtin is not enough of a Foucauldian social constructionist to say that our discourses entirely script and control us; part of the struggle is *our own* against received discourses, to find internally persuasive utterance.

The category of speaking subject, acting as a shorthand, specifies one side of an exchange. In logic and in actuality, the category entails as a requirement that there are more sides, maybe many more. It need not, usually does not mean that the subject is a biographical person: the subject positions, or "propositions of 'subject'" (Michael Davidson), need only to use the grammatical markers of self, preeminently pronouns, to generate a virtual person the reader can identify.

So subject and discourse are not in contradiction, if we may define the speaking subject as being literature's propositions of subject in, for example, post-1945 American time or post-1945 Soviet time, invoking the details of national tradition.[27] Subject and discourse fit together, precisely because the concept of the speaking subject diversifies and multiplies the traditional human subject, displaces the untenable notion of the unified self without rendering the subject a hollow container for ideologies. In fact, counterdiscourse between West and East is always in the process of expressing what it knows of the language of control. We gain explanatory power when we bring together, in a stereoscopic way, the concepts of speaking subject and of counterdiscourse. What we better explain is the historical momentum and the speech genre of literary resistance to social power. We need not call this resistance imagination, freedom, or self in order to be able to grant this resistance its own power. As Marina Tsvetaeva writes, "The poet takes up her speech from afar"[28]—far enough to represent other social selves, other rhetorics.

Since dialogue is endless, Bakhtin's meaning is also an unfixing of meaning, and his speaking subject is not always private property. Before moving on to more individualistic Western examples, I would like to show a more collective speaking subject in a kind of poetry that was contemporary with Bakhtin in his later years—Russian and collective, dissident and collective. From the sixties to 1989, there existed in Russia a nontraditional poetry, unlike anything in the West in the way it pervaded all levels of the culture, where it was literally true that the text was the poet's own voice and inseparable from that voice. The guitar poetry of Galich, Okudzhava, and Vysotsky flourished from the mid-sixties to the eighties, made possible by a new technology, the tape recorder (*magnitofon*), and sent out by tape recorder publishing (*magnitizdat*) on thousands of machines off of tapes from live concerts. These were bards known to millions, singer-poets who employed emphatic repetitive rhythms and fairly simple stanza structure, and for whom personality, intonation, and the grain of the voice are central assumptions. The inherently problematic nature of the textual object, and of the speaking subject, was not an immediately pressing topic for listeners.

Bulat Okudzhava: melancholy, mildly ironic, antiwar, antibureaucracy, understating, only very occasionally caustic in satire. Aleksandr Galich: a patrician ironist, noble in tribute to earlier poets, an actor inventing low-life characters whose attitudes, official or antiofficial, are undermined in the uttering. Vladimir Vysotsky: take-it-to-the-limit wiseguy, mock-criminal, observer of contradictions. The novelist Vasily Aksyonov remembers the first performance of Okudzhava's "Black Tomcat" in the hall of the Moscow Energy Institute, autumn 1962:

> He hides a grin behind his whiskers,
> Darkness his shield
> All other cats sing and sob—
> This black cat stays silent.

Everyone knew who it was with the moustache, Stalin as a tomcat. Aksyonov says: "The audience of two thousand students rose to their feet in a burst of enthusiastic emotion. The guitarist seemed to them to be a harbinger of redemption from . . . degradation."[29] The treatment of all three singer-poets in the West, particularly Vysotsky in his famous "Wolf Hunt," which was danced by Baryshnikov in a solo in the film *White Nights*, is mainly as writers of uncensored songs of dissent, and, while in part correct, this is a predatory and reductive Cold War reading. The medium and the meaning are not highly sophisticated, but these poets reach into the oral reserves of Russian literary culture, where song has not been devalued to the degree one sees outside that nation.

The speech genre of guitar poetry, as Gerald Stanton Smith has shown, derives from several historical and cultural sources—gypsy song, middle-ground songs of a certain daring and oddity, criminal songs, labor camp songs, and reverse images of official war songs; shared cultural knowledge of these in the background inevitably influenced the way these song poets presented their own voices.[30] In Vysotsky, the boldest example, the wrenched, semidestroyed voice is a guarantee of vitality, honesty. Vysotsky plays on and against the official mass song to get the effect of truth—anarchic, sexy, anything but official, but never obscene. The guitar poets are no longer at work. They have imitators but no heirs. Their songs were possible only in the era after 1955 or so, when the tape recorder had been mass produced, but before the availability of Western rock music. When these poets flourished there existed a genuine popular song of tremendous flexibility and social pertinence and rhythmic genius, personal and populist at once, learned about its speech genre and many more genres. Guitar poetry's naturalizing, voice-loving aesthetics is produced by the convergence of a number of ideological discourses, as a constellation of counterdiscourse to the Soviet mass song.

Voice is metaphor of person.[31] Readers are quick to register and scan the smallest hint of the other's self in the other's utterance, and readers enjoy going into hunt procedure when hints are obscured. Literary reading is a vast ground for the practice and extension of these skills. Reading texts must bear some normal structural relationship to the everyday practice of reading people's emotions. In both cases we learn to interpret markers or surrogates of person. Taken as a normal process of understanding, with its active verb, the speaking subject is a category describing the normal accurate-enough-for-life registration of markers of self; the speaking subject is a grid over all of discourse whose immensity and power may be demonstrated across the history of poetry. Because the chain of mediation between a single poem and its own condition of possibility is too long and evanescent to follow, these are examples of the social moorings of poetry in a restricted sense. However, this textual society of pronouns is itself dateable, as the most basic notation of an era's realities of relationship; so reading dialogic utterances in poetry can prepare us for a more capacious return to the text's social conditions of possibility, and to history beyond literary history.

In the old ballads, who is it that speaks, "Ich am of Irlonde, / Ant of the holy londe / Of Irlonde"? We can never know, because the anonymous "I" has emerged from the nowhere of chronotope, before 1600, anterior to authorship. Nevertheless, the instant claim of existence, "I am," the archaic spelling, rhymes, and refrain, quickly turn to the "Good sire" addressee; these make a joyous claim to fellowship ("Come ant dance wit me") from the mists of Irish time, in seven short lines.

In Sir Thomas Wyatt's "They Flee from Me" (1557), the courtly speaker vaguely identifies the "They" who flee from him, but only specifies a "she" in the middle of the twenty-first line of a three stanza poem: a love-passage, with her questioning "softly" (the speaker names her intonation): "Dear heart, how like you this?" (line 14). We do not know who she is except by her actions in the past, sweetness turned to "newfangleness" (line 19); and the speaking subject is also puzzled by her in the last line, "I fain would know what she hath deserved" (line 21). The speaker shows himself vulnerable to women and to change, emphasizing his uneasiness at another level by angry rhetorical reversals and awkward meter and rhyme-sounds. A whole attitude toward experience is shown by means of a self-questioning, minimal dialogism.

Two other Renaissance love poems, Marlowe's "The Passionate Shepherd to his Love" and Raleigh's answering "Nymph's Reply to the Shepherd," both dating 1600, have imaginary speakers, who by virtue of the pastoral convention come from outside the court, but who nonetheless can speak in perfectly turned witty quatrains. Speaker to speaker, these are dialogic because within the implied fable, the shepherd's blandishments are rebutted by the nymph's disdain for a "honey tongue," and by her realistic account of the hardships of the countryside; but also, author-to-reader twice dialogic in Raleigh's parodic re-use of the earlier poem's stanza and refrain, in order to devalue its details and sentiments. Under the guise of the nominal innocent speakers, these are utterances, like all pastorals, about scholarship and love in a court society anxious to hide, even to forfeit, its own sophistication.

Shakespeare's Sonnet 73 (1609), "That time of year thou mayst in me behold," is one of the high Renaissance achievements of this kind of anxious I, who here uses metaphors of the autumn season to show disproportion with the addressee: "thou" in lines 1, 5, 9, and three times in lines 13–14, who will live to love and speak after the death of the metaphor maker. Unlikeness of age or gender brings anxiety, which is the spur to utterance to an intimate but still shadowy auditor. Distance, disproportion is the spur to speech and the spinning out of story. Shakespeare is supreme in these matters, because he gives the impression of being autobiographical while always, in many ways and at all levels of language, denying final identity with his speaker. The distance between the speaker and himself, which we wish as readers always to conflate, is equally part of the story of the poem's pleasure.

Although Dryden hardly knew the much younger and infinitely less accomplished Oldham, Dryden's "To the Memory of Mr. Oldham" (1684) succeeds in its pose of sincere grief, an effect achieved by direct address, classicizing exaggeration ("Marcellus of our tongue"), stately convention. Dignified couplets and well known gestures of eulogy very oddly carry more feeling because it seems as if deep emotion is being over-controlled by a too traditional speaking subject; but of course that is what is intended.

It seems a postulate of the speaking subject that simulation of feeling, or mistakes about feeling, produces more feeling in response even when we know about artful lies or mistakes. Blake in his 1790s *Songs of Innocence and Experience,* and Robert Browning in his 1840s dramatic monologues, trust the reader to be able to read with sympathy as well as to criticize voices (ancient bard, Renaissance duke) obviously not the author's. In Goldsmith's "Deserted Village" (1770), the village is not only killed by trade and luxury—also by the decline of the countryside. The pastoral genre is moribund; the voice of poetry is weakened. We know that Samuel Johnson wrote the final two couplets of the long poem, but early editions never let on. How does knowing that fact change our idea of the speaker and his argument? Edward Fitzgerald's *Rubaiyat of Omar Khayyam* (1859) is an enormously popular translation whose speaking subject manages to touch some vague Victorian longing, while also plunging readers across space and time, so they think they are experiencing the chronotope of Omar. Walt Whitman in "Out of the Cradle Endlessly Rocking" (1881) writes an elegy for a bird, where the bird itself articulately calls to a boy, in a poem where even the Atlantic ocean "whisper'd me" and is a speaking subject. What is the status of the "I" in Emily Dickinson's "I heard a fly buzz—when I died—"? This speaker is dead, presumably—; a solemn privilege, because she can inform us about her acts and feelings at the moment of dying. Sometimes the greatest utterances have impossible speaking subjects.

The Clash of Inner and Outer Speech

Bakhtin took literature as the main territory for his philosophical work because it is the most massive and historically continuous example of agonistic double-voicing, of what he called "discourse as the subject of discourse."[32] As we have seen, even within the speaking subject as the producer of such discourse, there is non-identity, a collision of forces that fight it out on the territory of every utterance. The presence of speech genres, historical period styles, formal properties of structure, and the like in a long list, influences literature toward truces and maskings-over that unify the warring forces within each speaking subject, each text.

Our second reading-enabling category, the idea of a clash of inner and outer speech, is not so open as the speaking subject to reintegration by truce. Like Bakhtin, I prefer to phrase it as a struggle. Now, perhaps only a few New Age or fundamentalist believers would separate a quietist or world-denying inner speech.

Inner speech is not talking minus sound, but a particular kind of speech act. It has nothing to do with the unconscious, or with the inexpressible. A starting definition might be "dialogue with oneself," but that is not adequate. The opposed term in Bakhtin's lexicon is "outsidedness" (vnenakhodimost') or "exotopy," which Slavists translate variously as "being located outside/external to," "external position," "extralocality." Since Lev Vygotsky's *Thought and Language* in 1934, inner speech has been a leading topic of research in Soviet psychology—far more than in the West; Vygotsky's twenties–thirties work is more explicitly developmental and social than Bakhtin's in this area, but they share the belief that inner speech develops from outer speech, that the dialogic word is equally strong and possible in inner as well as outer speech, and that the clash of inner and outer speech is part of the very definition of literary writing.[33]

Outer speech is in us, indeed from our earliest years forms us, but inner speech can, if we need it, become a running resistance and commentary. Michael Holquist in *Dialogism* (1990) grasps the essential point and phrases it directly when he refers to extreme cases, which he calls "pathologies"; too much outer and we're on the way to domination by the discourse of others, too much inner and we are on the way to fantasy, even madness. When it comes to Bakhtinian study of ordinary cases, Holquist finds an admirable phrase for the clash when he refers to "psychology with a new subject of analysis: the psyche not of the individual, but of the individual as striated by the social."[34]

This is a neglected topic in Bakhtin studies because there is no essay dedicated to inner speech by Bakhtin or members of his circle—just a number of scattered mentions, mostly only a sentence or page. But when these are connected, they make a coherent statement about the formation and actual content of inner speech, and the way it results from/returns to social processes.

The first step in such a reconstruction would be V. N. Voloshinov's long essay of the mid 1920s, "Literary Stylistics," which discusses inner speech as essential to a sociology of art: a remarkably subtle Marxist theory of creation. He summarizes this phase of the argument thus: the human being's "whole inner life is formed in dependence on the means of expressing it. Without inner speech there can be no consciousness, just as there is no outer speech without inner speech."[35] Voloshinov describes how social groups form writers, who then confront society as an "outer milieu"—as a reading public; so "if contradictions and conflicts between the inner and outer speech of the writer do arise, there are special social causes for this" (110). There are stages in this development toward artistic speech and readerly response, but after the process is started it does not move in only one direction. Outer is innered, inner is outered, because both inner and outer speech are oriented toward someone else, a listener: "The style of the inner speech should determine that of outer speech, although the latter does have a feedback effect on the former. . . . [I]nner speech brings life and sap to the outer speech as it is perceived and is being created, but at the same time it is itself determined by it" (110). Further in the essay, Voloshinov speaks of the dialogic character of inner speech, "totally saturated with the evaluations of the possible listener or audience, even if the speaker has no idea whatever of this listener" (118). Dominated by official norms, monologic inner speech is conditioned by social class. But dialogic inner speech may be conditioned by "two equally powerful voices": here, as sometimes happens in the utterance of heroes in Dostoevsky, dialogic inner speech is "marked [by] the clash within the *one* speech flow of the *two* ideologies, the two points of view of the warring classes" (119–20; emphasis in *Bakhtin School Papers*). A member of a declining class may drop out of his or her class environment, "out of the social sphere" (120), go outside social expression in language, in which case it is possible that *the sexual becomes a surrogate* (a counterfeit and substitute) *for the social*" (121; emphasis in *Bakhtin School Papers*). The translation has "sexual," but the larger discussion makes clear that Voloshinov means "physiological" or "biological," with this meaning: when individuals lose faith in their possible historical significance, they reroute all cycles through the body (sex and death). In a period of crisis or decline, the writer may show how this breakdown of language and society occurs by forcing into the open the conflict of inner and outer speech (120–21).

Bakhtin and members of his circle had more to say on inner speech than on the other three categories I have chosen. What they say is fascinating; briefly I want to suggest the range of their thought on inner speech, in passages dated from the 1920s to the 1950s; on occasion I will intervene with my own comments.

1928: from Pavel Medvedev, *The Formal Method in Literary Scholarship*, two passages: "Even the inner utterance (interior speech) is social; it is oriented toward a possible audience, toward a possible answer, and it is only in the process of such an orientation that it is able to take shape and form." And: "To say that we think in words, along in a stream of inner speech, is to fail to clearly realize what this means. For we do not think in words and sentences, and the stream of inner speech which flows within us is not a string of words and sentences. We think and conceptualize in utterances, complexes complete in themselves."[36] The indispensable article on this topic, one of the truly profound studies in the literature on Bakhtin, is Caryl Emerson's "The Outer Word and Inner Speech," where she concludes: "These, then, are the ways an awareness of the gap between inner and outer might function in both life and literature: as an index of individual consciousness, as a measure of our escape from fixed plots and roles, as a prerequisite for discourse itself."[37] Of course, even while testing a relationship, the individual is always in a minimal rapport with the other, and inner speech as a pre-requisite for discourse already contains some forms of discourse.

Inner speech has been a great theme of Russian psychology since the 1930s when Vygotsky said that it consists entirely of predicates, and since the 1950s when Zhinkin said that it lacks the redundancy inherent in all natural languages—that is, inner speech when not controlled is extremely fast and condenses, using images, schemata, symbols, and phonetic fragments. Bakhtin and Vygotsky agree on the rhetorical form of inner speech: for them it might look like short antiphonal lines of dialogue. More recent Russian experimental psychologists have been able to test some of these hunches by clever experiments involving close measuring, but the furthest experiments we know are literary: Proust's long sentences as curves of thought, and Molly Bloom's gargantuan unpunctuated sentences of soliloquy in Joyce's *Ulysses*.

1929 (revised version 1963): In *Problems of Dostoevsky's Poetics*, in two passages Bakhtin writes: "Alyosha's words, intersecting with Ivan's inner speech, must be juxtaposed to the words of the devil, which also repeat the words and thoughts of Ivan himself." And, on the Underground Man: "He cannot reach an agreement with himself, but neither can he stop talking with himself. The style of his discourse about himself is organically alien to the [punctuational] period, alien to finalization, both in its separate aspects and as a whole. This is the style of internally endless speech which can be mechanically cut off but cannot be organically completed."[38] In Dostoevsky's *The Brothers Karamazov* but also in lyric or dramatic works, characters can repeat or distort the inner speech of other characters, in intentional resonance, not always ironic: one thinks of the anti-petrarchanism of Mercutio in Shakespeare's *Romeo and Juliet*, where he mocks Romeo's conventional love of Rosalind. A character can be overheard, like the speaker in *Notes from the Underground*, speaking to himself obsessively; or the speaker can be confessionally wounding himself, taunting the silent addressee, as in Browning's "Fra Lippo Lippi."

1934–35: "Discourse in the Novel": After quoting from a novel by Turgenev Bakhtin says: "Here we have . . . a form of a character's quasi-direct discourse. . . . Judging by its syntactic markers, it is authorial speech, but its entire emotional structure belongs to Nezhdanov. This is his inner speech, but transmitted in a way regulated by the author. . . . Such a form for transmitting inner speech is common in Turgenev (and is generally one of the most widespread forms for transmitting inner speech in the novel). This form introduces order and stylistic symmetry into the disorderly and impetuous flow of a character's inner speech (a disorder and impetuosity would otherwise have to be reprocessed into direct speech), and, moreover, through its syntactic (third-person) and basic stylistic markers. . . . Such form permits another's inner speech to merge, in an organic and structured way, with a context belonging to the author."[39] This would have been impossible within the form of indirect discourse. Here, as elsewhere, Bakhtin allows the language of narrative to approach some of the conditions of the language of lyric, in the disguised advancing of the author's voice.

1952–53: In "The Problem of the Text," an essay in *Speech Genres*, Bakhtin writes: "The event of the life of the text, that is, its true essence, always develops on the boundary between two consciousnesses, two subjects." "The unique nature of dialogic relations. The problem of the inner dialogism."[40] One possible limitation of the inner dialogism, more prevalent in poetry, is: what if the dialogue with the self turns in the same circle, begins to race or to rationalize unduly? How does one still the inner dialogue by clearing the mind? Bakhtin never took a direct interest in the role of meditation as an extra refinement of inner speech—bio- or neuro-feedback, the quieting *of* inner speech *by* inner speech. But what he did say is mightily suggestive, and may be extended through examples, to help the reader be more alert to the social striation of inner speech.

One definition of poetry: dialogism driven somewhat further inward than in prose narrative.

The clash of inner and outer speech is evident within each stanza of anonymous ballads like "The Sparrow Hawk's Complaint." The refrain in Latin, "Timor mortis conturbat me," is the bird's death-obsessed statement, which she teaches to the unknown I who uses it out of quotation marks to start the utterance; and which rhymes with I's own lines in English. Is it outering or innering of inner speech? There is not enough evidence to decide—a deliberate effect. Whether I meets dread in the bird, or projects it onto the bird, we cannot know. The elements of utterance are simple, sturdy; the effect is far from simple.

Samuel Daniel's Sonnet 46 in his *Delia* sequence (1592) begins by contrasting his own lively speech of living praise, "But I must sing of thee and those fair eyes" (line 5), with conventional exaggerations: "Let others sing of knights and paladins / In aged accents of untimely words" (lines 1–2). The claim of naturalness is here becoming a trope of naturalness, as Daniel actually uses the anticonventional code word: "Authentic shall my verse in time to come" (line 6). After twelve lines of self-praise, he makes a final-couplet concession that takes the preening one further step: "Though th'error of my youth they shall discover, / Suffice, they show I lived and was thy lover." The clash of inner and outer speech shows up in this lover's high concern for the authenticity of his own rhetoric, in the middle of his seductive praises.

The speech of religion may also contain a struggle, as in Donne's violent metaphors for religious rapture in "Batter my heart" (c. 1609) or in George Herbert's more utterance-based idea of prayer in "The Collar" (1633). Herbert's poem opens with thirty-two lines of quoted inner speech, resisting his own faith, but turns against itself and back to faith in the final quatrain: "But as I raved and grew more fierce and wild, / At every word, / Methought I heard one calling, *Child!* / And I replied, *My Lord.*" Denial turns dramatically into the underlying acceptance in the speaker who is himself a collar-wearing minister of the church by means of a brief but conclusive dialogue between the true, apparently outer God and the straying inner self. The convention of "*Methought*" is Herbert's way to outer what is inner, by means of the medieval phrase for allowable, counterfactual perception; the convention of italics is Herbert's way to show by typography an entirely different mode of utterance, one not needing quotation marks because it shows outer and inner speech are at one in prayer.

There is another last-moment reversal at the end of Milton's "Lycidas" (1637), where in the final verse paragraph the poet announces "Thus sang the uncouth swain to th'oaks and rills!" We had thought it was learned Milton-in-guise-of-shepherd, lamenting his friend's death and making a stocktaking of his own life and career as a writer, but it was someone else, an uncouth swain singing not writing! It is a conventional reframing, but the movement from inner speech to outer at this point is breathtaking. The abandonment of one speaker forces a reassessment of the previous 185 lines: how could that lofty Christian classicism come from an uncouth swain? And who speaks the final eight lines? We cannot know, but there is a magnificent tone of haughty cruelty here, in the dismissal of speaker, poem, and reader.

The clash of inner and outer speech is the armature of Wordsworth's sonnet, "Surprised by Joy" (1815), which begins by addressing an impossible auditor, Caroline his daughter, dead three years. There follow two exclamations and two rhetorical questions, seemingly addressed to himself as well as to Caroline, who is treated less directly in the poem's final lines ("my heart's best treasure" [line12]; "that heavenly face" [line14]). He cannot keep his grief for her pure, and joy has overtaken him; but a huge word, "vicissitude" in line 4 has already, though covertly, revealed his own concern about death. The poem's occasion is the natural slackening, and the attempt through memory to return to the original pitch, of grief; but this most intimate topic evokes one even more hidden, the speaker's fear of annihilation. This countertopic is not surprising, because this is the inner speech of all Wordsworth's inner speech; it does not clash with the Caroline-grief theme but seems rather to render that public by comparison, a tender guise for an obsession.

Other Romantic and Victorian poems may be read for these clashes. Coleridge's meditative "Frost at Midnight" (1798) has the typical rondo-structure of greater Romantic lyrics: outer turn to frost, inward turn to meditation and memory, concluding outer turn in the address to the nearby "Dear Babe" in relation to the "secret ministry of frost" outside (line 72). Coleridge's first and longer version of "Dejection: An Ode" (1802) is addressed to one dear auditor, and the second is cast in more formal stanzas without a continuous stated auditor, though sections 4 and 5 address a mysterious Lady; so taken together the versions change purposes and methods as they change audiences, the latter a public and censored version of the former, brilliantly edited: revision is usually an outering. "Do I wake or sleep?" at the end of Keats's "Ode to a Nightingale" is a larger statement of the clash; so too the cross-purposes in Elizabeth Barrett Browning's "A Musical Instrument," which pits song against life, and in Longfellow's "Fire of Driftwood," which sets poet against man, "making a poet out of a man." Tennyson takes up the failure of outer speech in "Break, Break, Break," when he admits, "I would that I could utter / The thoughts that arise in me": I would that I could outer. Matthew Arnold in "The Buried Life" finds inner speech not adequate to stand against the force of public opinion, and here as in his "Dover Beach," he gestures to a nearby woman who might understand more than the clamoring crowd.

Emily Dickinson, always most searching about these matters of utterance and innering, speaks of "internal difference / Where the meanings, are" ("There's a certain slant of light"). I would add the corollary, implied in her lines: no internal difference without a prior clash between outer and inner. This phrasing of Dickinson's, generated in a poem about the inarticulate fore-sense of death, is as profound a sketch of the divisions on the territory of the utterance as anything in Bakhtin.

Intonation

Intonation in an utterance permits the hearer/reader to identify, and if necessary disentangle, the social languages involved, including feeling-tones of intent. It works best in face-to-face communication, but intonation may be coded into, and read back from, written utterances. As I have shown, Bakhtin and Voloshinov described the preeminently social nature of tones in speech: tone of voice is a relationship, and is often to be described by emotion-names and adverbs such as "vindictive," or "prattling," "intense," or leisurely, but also to be described by listing the otherness, or conflict, that has determined the tone. On the wavering border between the verbal and the nonverbal, intonation acts as an interconnector, an emotional shorthand. It is devilish to read in a literary context because there is nothing tell-tale in vocabulary, syntax, metrical properties, length of units, or special sounds, which can be codified. Intonation requires that we be quick, omnivorous, and subtle on the uptake, and this means it is easy to fall into mistakes about social tones. This ad hoc, unpinnable, nonstructural quality of intonation is probably the reason why it is often avoided in linguistic and literary study: applied locally but rarely considered in its social range, rarely applied to whole utterances, whole works.

Dwight Bollinger is a linguist who has given intelligent attention to this topic, treating intonation, the "Cinderella of the communication complex," as a kind of gesture, where cultural language has "traveled the least distance of all."[41] But in his "first things first" approach to pitch change, stressing, and music in speech, Bollinger admits he will not face intonation as a fully cultural dimension of language. Bollinger the renegade linguist consciously risks reductionism, while Bakhtin the philosopher insisting on cultural language, risks making claims too large.

Intonation, for Bakhtin and members of his circle, requires a method that resolves words, sentences, and devices into larger and more variable kinds of units: into social and dialogic utterances. Voloshinov in the 1920s spoke of the relation between local instance and overall design, when lyric intonation enlists the reader's sympathy and when an intonational metaphor is built up by repeating similar devices across an utterance. Bakhtin himself in the 1920s referred to "emotional-volitional tone" in his treatise on *The Philosophy of the Act*, meaning explicitly to stiffen or dignify the emotional with personal agency. In her review of the English translation of this treatise, Caryl Emerson calls "emotional-volitional tone" the "proper clamp between culture and life," referring to the passage in the book where Bakhtin explains how, as soon as I experience my experience as my own, tone permeates my actions. Later, in the 1950s and 1960s, Bakhtin was again writing about "expressive intonation," which he was still defining as belonging to the utterance and not to the single word.[42]

Juliet Flower MacCannell and Stefania Sini have, from their different viewpoints, coordinated and commented upon these kinds of statements in Bakhtin, emphasizing intonation as the uttered evidence of a shared interpretation of a state of affairs: Intonation as Figure, in MacCannell's phrase.[43] Writing in the mid 1980s, MacCannell proposes that if Bakhtin's message is to be taken in full seriousness, "sociologists will have to become good writers—and literary critics will have to become good sociologists," and this because everyone concerned with discourse needs to become attentive to what is fought out on the territory of the utterance. To a degree, this has happened in the years since MacCannell wrote, at least on the side of critics as sociologists. MacCannell explains, "By the same token that intonation can give 'life' to an abstract entity, it also allows the mutual reverse: that what is living (values) can be struck dumb (or dead) by virtue of form. In verbal discourse, that is, 'healthy social value judgements' are basically 'represented' smuggling 'life' into the dead alien word of language, and 'death' into the presence of the life of the word" (984). On the inescapably social territory of the utterance, the stakes in this translinguistics are high: nothing less than death and life of the word.

Bakhtin has much to say about intonation, in several places over many years, but very few examples. I should say that in a practical, local way, intonation correlates the acts of utterance to social norms and preferences; intonation, since it performs this, is one of the always-present social moorings of poetry to society. This most remarkably and often occurs when there is a change of intent in the speaker—when, for example, a speaker wishes to inaugurate an utterance, or when it is time for the speaker to shift to another attitude to the addressee at the close of the section and poem. (There are obviously many other prominent and less prominent places for a change of direction and attitude—and for a change of speakers.) Across the whole work, there may be one dominant intonation, dictated by the speech genre that the writer has chosen: it is in such definitions that intonation verges on the next and more global category, the image of a language. But in our sequential reading practice, intonation marks a shift both local and temporary.

Thomas Wyatt's "My Lute, Awake!" (1557), for example, begins by addressing and waking the instrument (stanza 1), which stands for poetry and seduction. But in the middle stanzas (4–7) the addressee has become the resistant woman—spoken to in attitudes of intimidation, heady praise, and carpe diem blandishment. The speaker is angry at the person he hopes to win over! And he mixes anger with seemingly contradictory emotions as part of his campaign. Then in the final stanza (8) he marks his failure by returning to his lute, his talent: "Now cease, my lute. This is the last / Labor that thou and I shall waste." In the three-stage argument, frustration

and bitterness and anger take over; two changes of addressee inten-
sify, and mixtures of emotion complicate, the social tone. Of the
thousands of love-complaint poems written in 1557, this is the one
anthologized and rightly admired, because the intensity and compli-
cation of tone produce a reality-effect within a gridwork otherwise
perfectly conventional.

In "Jordan (I)" (1633), George Herbert asks questions for two
stanzas, wondering if there may be truths that are beautiful in themselves without needing stock images and sound patterns: pastoral
and riddling fictions are fine, but not his way to pray. He ends: "Nor
let them punish me with loss of rhyme, / Who plainly say, *My God,
My King.*" The intonation-word is "plainly," the poem's only adverb,
saved to point to a value in the final line and to prepare the italicized
prayer that ends the utterance by shifting typeface and addressee. It
is typical of Herbert to run a poem's logic in one direction and then
to reverse or transcend that, just in closing. Change from human to
divine addressee, here as there, is saved for the end and marked by
many devices, including a shift in tone from darkly speculative to
joyously devotional. That he requires social tones to escape social
tones, and in the midst of denying them, is the paradox of Herbert's
last-words prayer.

A satire like Dryden's "MacFlecknoe" (1682) pumps up a heroic
balloon by many images and sounds of pompous glory, but must
never admit that over-praise is condemnation. The reader who is in
the know will see through the surface praise that is addressed directly to the victim, "Thou last great prophet of tautology," Thomas
Shadwell. The ironic tone is modulated through thousands of details and effects in 217 lines of couplets, and through the mocking
narrative of passing on the mantle of dullness, but there are no
major tonal shifts. The point is to enjoy a continuous joke of attitude
that has begun with the choice of satire, as a mock-heroic speech-
genre, which does not mock the heroic but what the heroic has become.[44]

Also lacking a major modulation of tone is Jonathan Swift's tale
in octosyllabics, "The Lady's Dressing Room" (1730), which takes
Strephon through Celia's room to find things that contradict her
pose of feminine aloofness. The list is ordered in crescendo, so that
the shepherd lad may make a logical summation: "finishing his
grand survey, / Disgusted Strephon stole away / Repeating in his
amorous fits, / Oh, Celia, Celia, Celia shits!" The tone is named:

"Disgusted." The scatological vision and the sense of offended smell come in the latter sections of Swift's works, when rhetoric and reality are forced furthest apart. The violence of misogyny here matches the violence of misanthropy in the fourth voyage of *Gulliver's Travels*, so energetic is he, that perhaps (as Robert Elliott has suggested) Swift's images undermine the social order he is so concerned to support. In making satire work at a level almost tragic, Swift's literary skill is actively at odds with his conservative politics. Some tones even he, literary history's greatest ventriloquist of invented personas, cannot control.

The assignment for writer and reader in Augustan poems is often how to manage and justify arriving at a moral conclusion, as in Johnson's "Vanity of Human Wishes" where images of aimless rising and falling must give way to a question about ultimate ends; "Where then shall hope and fear their objects find?" Johnson's grave, declaratory unity of tone and intent is very possible in the Romantic and Victorian periods, but with the break of eras in 1795, questions of tone do become more problematic. In a more avant-garde or exploratory or meditative poetry, social tones may sometimes seem not to touch the words, and we begin to find perplexities of over and under statement.

At the end of the magnificent "Tintern Abbey" (1798), Wordsworth wobbles. At line 120 of 160, we discover with some surprise that there has been all along a nearby addressee who is not ourselves, namely his sister Dorothy. When he turns to "My dear, dear Sister!" in this last verse paragraph, he picks up a more preachy but more uncertain rhetoric of negative affirmations, rhetorical questions, gentle commands, exclamations, assertions, lists, and rhetorical turns at dash-broken lines and breaks between lines. Wordsworth's anxiety about the continuity of his personality, and his disgusted ever-present concern with his own death, here lead him to treat Dorothy with some condescension. Rousing the reader's worries, this complicates but does not impugn the poem's struggle for meaning.

The extreme opposite case in Wordsworth's century is Swinburne, who in the choruses from *Atalanta in Calydon* (1865) or in the shorter lines of "The Garden of Proserpine" (1866), produces a languid drone from perfect rhymes, heavy alliteration, and rhythms of energetic lassitude, so that there may seem to be no meaning at all to struggle for: intonation nearly without content, or at any rate without argument or perceptual acuity. There is much intoning in Edgar Allan Poe's "The Raven" (1845), where the trapped speaker increases the uncanniness through heavy repetition and refrain, but Poe's speaker unlike Swinburne's has a modulation to close in the final stanza's shift to present tense verbs; also Poe's speaker himself learns at last to say, and not merely quote, the Raven's one-tone "Nevermore."

As much as satirical social tones are typical of the period style of eighteenth-century Augustans, one mark of the century of Wordsworth and Poe is uneasiness with social tones, indeed with human society. (Rejection of, or incompetence with, social tones plainly has its own social moorings, which relate to the writer's increasing sense of being on the margins of an industrial society, with its objectification of experience.) Hence the poems on birds like Poe's, or like Whitman's "Out of the Cradle" with a bird's song called an "aria," or Matthew Arnold's "Philomela," where the feeling-tones of bird song are praised more explicitly than anywhere else: "Eternal passion! / Eternal pain!" Oddly in Whitman and Arnold, so different in other ways as literary figures, both seek feeling rather than unfeeling, aware of mid-century loss of affect in violent cities of the industrial age; and both find quintessence of feeling in bird speech. This is a small instance of a larger condition, showing how the social moorings of poetry in the nineteenth century are historically different than in other eras; eager to experience the feeling behind all possible tones, many poets, including the best, are less adept at social tones than writers of earlier Augustan and later Modernist eras. Wobbling of tone is as worth hearing as assurance, from the point of view of the reader who is mapping struggles upon the territory of the utterance.

The Image of a Language

The fourth and last of these terms, which I am taking from Mikhail Bakhtin's defense of fiction but elaborating for poetry, is something he arrives at in the act of working out a philosophy of speaking persons in narrative. This comes quite far along in his best methodological piece on fiction, "Discourse in the Novel," when he is showing how "the speaking person in the novel need not necessarily be incarnated in a character." The speaking subject may also appear in parodic stylizations or, Bakhtin says, in the form of inserted genres, posited authors or *skaz*. This last-listed Russian genre term can be applied to stories in all languages, where provincial narrators tell the whole story including dialogue in idiosyncratic or dialect speech.

How to transmit and assess the speech of others? For Bakhtin, it is not enough to speak of "stylization," though that is part of the problem, and the *skaz* practitioners and the French and German philological students of *style indirect libre* have done valuable studies on discourse as the subject of discourse. Bakhtin takes forty pages to unfold his thought on how we might be more adequate with his new term, but the central passage would seem to be here, at first mention of the term:

> All these languages—even when they are not incarnated in a character—have been made socially and historically concrete and to one degree or another have become reified—only a single and unitary language, one that does not acknowledge other languages alongside itself, can be subject to reification—and therefore the images of speaking persons, clothed in the specifics of a given society in a given point in history, show through behind them. Characteristic for the novel as a genre is not the image of a man in his own right, but a man who is precisely the *image of a language*. But in order that language become an artistic image, it must become speech from speaking lips, conjoined with the image of a speaking person.
>
> If the subject making the novel specifically a novel is defined as a speaking person and his discourse, striving for social significance and a wider general application as one distinctive language in a heteroglot world—then the central problem for stylistics of the novel may be formulated as the problem of *artistically representing language, the problem of representing the image of a language.*[45]

We may guess, from context, that it is the author's first task to make formal devices of speech account for multiple consciousnesses, language intentions, voices, and accents: implying or showing the way another's words are other, organizing many speakers to reply to one another, and finding a style to superintend all that.

For the author, it is a matter of large executive choices that determine the smallest changes in rhetoric and tone. It is next the commentator's problem—not to apply the received terms of rhetoric in such a way as to lose the import of another's speech, or the determining role of the big original choices of pre-writing about who speaks and how.

The exact reproduction of another's word, as in something like a tape recording, is of little interest to Bakhtin; rather in this study he wishes to describe "the double-voiced *representation* of another's word in the novel with its orientation toward *the image of a language*," which means that "the other's words must undergo special artistic reformulation." But what reformulation? Bakhtin is never explicit on this topic, but only hints that novelistic hybrids merge the individual element with the sociological element (360), and that there may be a system of the images of a language (416). The mutual illumination of languages would seem to have an intentionality of its own: an art-intention. Bakhtin names this intention, at its highest and most dialogic expression, fiction. But he does in this essay give a small opening to poetry, when near the end he allows that "of special importance is the re-accentuation of poetic images into prosaic ones, and vice versa" (421).

The image of a language is the most obscure of these four categories. The phrase itself yokes what is seen and what is heard, what is particular and what is abstract. My attempt to use the term must struggle against Anglo-American practical opportunism and the resistance to generality. Perhaps too the term's acceptance is made harder by the Russian tongue's rather different ways of displaying the meaning of the term *image*. Russian *obraz* means shape, form, appearance, image, type, figure, mode, manner, way, or icon; and the cognate *obrazovanie* means formation or education. In English as in Russian, the image is both the object under study and the reduced representation of that object; but Russian emphasizes somewhat more the imaginative and form-making process, and the co-presence of thing and thought.

The image of a language, in my expansion of Bakhtin's definitions, is a framing category for marking off mid-level collective utterances: characterizations of kinds of languages that are smaller than national languages, yet larger than personal idiolects or styles of single works. We can only have the image of a language if there are other languages, differentially defined against the one we have isolated. If we read for the image of languages in a literary or other work, we sensitize ourselves to the ways of speaking of social groups.

So the image of a language is a global framing of other themes, and may be understood as organizing the speaking subject, inner speech, and intonation. That is why we come to it after the expositions of those terms. Some of its elements, taken up by Bakhtin, are internally persuasive discourse externally validated, the "dialogic penetration into the word" in various professions and disciplines (352), the way rhetorical genres may be dialogized into speech genres, dialect in relation to received standard speech, the hybridization of languages. Not, then, just a matter of idiolect or one person's special way of utterance, but of sociolect, language-types or social-linguistic registers, relative to other types or registers; but more, too, the artistic representation of a sociolect.

If we need proof that the image of language is useful for poetry, *The Canterbury Tales* is a transcendent work of poetry with jostling images of English.[46] This example is also useful for the overall argument, because Chaucer is writing an inter-genre between narrative and poetry. Chaucer's pilgrims, as different as Wife of Bath and Pardoner, have different vocabularies, life histories, and moral visions, though all are represented as remembered by the overall narrator, Chaucer, who records utterance in elegantly turned couplets.

Minor examples of images of a language occur in quoted speech in poems, something Thomas Wyatt specializes in. There is the famous half-line sentence from a woman, "Dear heart, how like you this?" in "They flee from me." Wyatt also has the switch away from a jealous male speaker to the splendid couplet-long collar inscription on the neck of the female deer, in "Whoso List to Hunt," which ends that poem, "*Noli me tangere*, for Caesar's I am, / And Wild for to hold, though I seem tame." Hands off the monarch's woman!! seems to be the implied allegory; if that guess is correct, Wyatt stunningly moors his lyric in the circumstance of court society.

Larger and more encompassing examples occur in poems organized by particular speech genres, such as apostrophe poems like Raleigh's "To His Son" or Donne's "The Sun Rising," which begins "Busy old fool, unruly sun, / Why dost thou thus." There are also wisdom poems like Thomas Nashe's "Litany in Time of Plague" and Robert Frost's "Provide, Provide."

A sonnet is a kind of speech genre, not in its guise as a poem of fourteen lines with a certain rhyme scheme, but in its traditional subject matters and rhetorics. When the sonnet is developed into sequences in the Early Modern period, and reimagined by uncommon philosophical reach and rhetorical brio in Shakespeare, the seemingly trivial form takes on a new narrative role, as the image of a capacious language. A similar argument might be made for the transformation of the ballad-stanza and the ballad-content in the

Romantic era, in the landmark genre-title *Lyrical Ballads* and what it implies about developing folk utterance into high-art utterance by lyricizing it.

For Milton, taking genre as image of a language in "Lycidas" meant that he could employ the pastoral for a personal testimony of his own poetic unreadiness, and for an attack on immoral leaders in the English church. For Samuel Johnson, in his "Life of Milton" a century later, pastoral is easy and artificial, so Milton's poem is a disaster—unreadable because an image of an impossible, passé language.

Phillis Wheatley, author of "On Being Brought from Africa to America" (1773), wrote with all the complex conventions of Augustan poetry but changed the vocabulary and attitudes, finding the image of a Black language and selfhood within existing American English. It meant very directly (but also with genial tact) criticizing in her poems the existing image of English, and also inventing another English within English where her color and life, and her poetic identity, could flourish.

John Keats shows the most intelligent understanding of the image of a language in the English tradition. He worked through the manners and materials of Leigh Hunt, Wordsworth, Milton, and Shakespeare in sequence, boldly appropriating styles and their social meanings, and then moving on to more inclusive styles. One by one he exactly caught and then surpassed the whole intent of his predecessors. Then in "To Autumn" near the end of his writing life, he found a language of process for a personified season—as if Autumn could think.

Victorian poets learned this kind of imaginative appropriation from the Romantics: Browning's early imitation and quick horrified rejection of Shelley's personal manner; Tennyson's image of an epic Latin style in "To Virgil" ("stateliest measure / Ever moulded by the lips of man" is the poem's conclusive image of a language); Arnold's yearning for cultural cohesion in his sonnet, "Shakespeare." William Butler Yeats caught on to a reigning period style of Pre-Raphaelite sweet sounds and images of interiority, in Victorian period poems such as "The Lake Isle of Innisfree," but then after 1900 chastened his style by writing for the theater and by putting politics into poems. Yeats found a plain-speaking style in midcareer to use for themes relating to Irish nationalism and chaotic modernity. In the very late "Under Ben Bulben" (1939), the epitaph he proposes

for himself at poem's end is italicized for emphasis: "*Cast a cold eye /
On life, on death. / Horseman, pass by!*" These are metaphors for a language beyond convention, even beyond judgment and morality and
life; images of a nonspatial, synaesthetic language, cold for touch
plus eye for sight, a language that might come from the other side
of death. This "cold eye" is the apt final image of my survey, because
it is utterance imagining removing itself from the territory of utterance.

Yeats's "cold eye" is, very likely, the furthest reach of any image
of a language, typical of modernity and postmodernity but not
within the ken of a theorist of communication like Bakhtin. Nonetheless, it is Bakhtin's category of the image of a language that has
brought us to the point of surpassing Bakhtin.

2

Bakhtin and the Social Poetics of Dialect

Two Examples of Dialect Poetry

WHAT WOULD HAPPEN IF WE TOOK DIALECT WRITING AS SERIOUSLY AS those who write in dialect, if we wanted to think past dialect as archaic or local in the sense of pious nostalgia? My account of the way language helps to form cultural identity in Glasgow-Scots and London-Caribbean dialect, in their relation to the majority language of standard English, contributes to the creation of a scholarship of interculture for our moment, a scholarship derived from studies of postcolonial writing sites, transgressive border and diaspora cultures, foreign natives. To declare my argument and method right away: against the likely false consciousness in overstrong forms of nationalist ideology, as expressed in the English Only constitutional amendment proposed in the United States and in the political use of received standard pronunciation in the United Kingdom, I will connect Mikhail Bakhtin's philosophy of social heteroglossia to the centrifugal, entropic energies of dialect writing. The idea is to make a small, stubborn, non-nostalgic reference to the local and the plural.

As the need at the moment in a social study of the languages of English is not for survey but for theoretical advance, my textual base is small, but I shall work it hard and shall privilege it by full quotation. The first of my two study texts is "Unrelated Incident (3)" by Tom Leonard of Glasgow:[1]

> this is thi
> six a clock
> news thi
> man said n
> thi reason
> a talk wia

BBC accent
is coz yi
widna wahnt
mi ti talk
aboot thi
trooth wia
voice lik
wanna yoo
scruff.if
a toktaboot
thi trooth
lik wanna yoo
scruff yi
widny thingk
it wuz troo.
jist wanna yoo
scruff tokn.
thirza right
way ti spell
ana right way
ti tok it.this
is me tokn yir
right way a
spellin.this
is ma trooth.
yooz doant no
thi trooth
yirsellz cawz
yi canny talk
right.this is
the six a clock
nyooz.belt up.[2]

The second poem is "It dread inna Inglan" by Linton Kwesi Johnson of London; as I present it in printed form, it is necessary to say
that the poem is most fully encountered in its recorded version, spoken by the poet to a reggae beat:

dem frame-up George Lindo
up in Bradford Toun
but di Bradford Blacks
dem a rally roun
mi seh dem frame-up George Lindo

>up in Bradford Toun
>but di Bradford Blacks
>dem a rally roun. . . .
>
>Maggi Tatcha on di go
>wid a racist show
>but a she haffi go
>kaw,
>rite now,
>African
>Asian
>West Indian
>an' Black British
>stan firm inna Inglan
>inna disya time yah
>far noh mattah wat dey say,
>come wat may,
>we are here to stay
>inna Inglan,
>inna disya time yah. . . .
>
>George Lindo
>him is a working man
>George Lindo
>him is a family man
>George Lindo
>him nevah do no wrong
>George Lindo
>di innocent one
>George Lindo
>him noh carry no daggah
>George Lindo
>him is nat no rabbah
>George Lindo
>dem haffi let him go
>George Lindo
>dem bettah free him now![3]

I set these out early, so that their full strangeness-in-familiarity of sound and rhythm may modify my context-building, and stand as evidence for the analytical grapple.

The theory of dialect is a theory of glossaries, which need not by their presence reinforce the idea of local writing as alien or defective. From the writer's point of view, dialect is always, as orthography, a notation; usually it means the writer's invention of the image of the speech of another. The theory of dialect is also a theory of glossolalia, at least in the sense that the partial bafflement of the standard speaker-reader is intended. The uncanniness of the sounds and syntax will violate and restructure the table of values, coming as these effects do from another site within the same language. Dialect writers are scholars of sounds, rhythms. Chirographic and conventional their scripts may be, but the marks of the image of the oral on this writing are shocking to the standard reader, so different is this printed voice, so unassimilable and yet still English. It is a case where the least difference has more significance than there would be if another language entirely were used. Dialect writing, like all literary writing, forces the reader to reproduce it exactly in the mind, on the vocal cords.

Socially and dialogically, to bring in terms from Bakhtin, the crucial thing about dialect poetry is that we inhabit the others' speech, *chuzhaia rech'*, but beyond that we inhabit—in the sense of *sobytie*, being with or identifying with—the actual rebarbative sounds. The rest is lexis and prosody. In principle, reading this poetry is the same kind of literary experience as reading a heavily elaborated diction in Alexander Pope, or reading a special avant-garde language like Gertrude Stein's *Tender Buttons*. Usually, though my examples from Leonard and Kwesi Johnson are exceptions, these poets are formally so traditional that it is as if modernism had not occurred. They exhaust their imaginativeness in the creation of an orthography, and in the determined programmatic wish to overturn the elite pretensions of standard English. Often they discuss the overweening authority of official English, refuting a language-politics in argument as well as by means of sound.

In its orientation toward oral speech, dialect poetry is the *skaz* (loosely, colloquial narrative) of the poetic mode. It is a low-down speech-genre that defamiliarizes the standard or official from within or beneath. From this derives its possible relation to a Bakhtinian politics of carnival, for Bakhtin in his Rabelais study elected to write the story of discourses outside power. Beyond a focus on puns and body language, Marxist and liberationist accounts of Bakhtin, which make the Rabelais book central, have not touched on the book's eloquent pages on the explosion of vernaculars in Rabelais's historical

moment. The issue of dialect is central here. I do see a shift in Bakhtin's use of the term *dialect* (same in Russian, *dialekt*) between his
twenties–thirties meaning and the point, thirty and more years later,
when he rises to the conclusion of *Rabelais and His World* (1965). In
the Bakhtin-school study on *The Formal Method in Literary Scholarship*
(1928), Viktor Shklovsky is trounced for "naïve confusion of the linguistic definition of language . . . of dialectological characteristics
(Church Slavonicisms, popular dialects) with the poetic functions of
language."[4] I count twenty-one uses of *dialect* and *dialectological* in
the 1934–35 essay, "Discourse in the Novel," and its contextual
reach makes one feel the term nearby during the first three-fourths
of the essay even when the word itself is absent. Dialect in these early
studies is either natural language or the "abstract-linguistic" account of it,[5] but it may rarely enter into the realm of style.

In the Rabelais study, Bakhtin identifies new social forces with ver-
nacular languages and sees not only the "interorientation of three
languages" in Rabelais but also the co-presence of "national folk idioms . . . the artistic search for dialectalisms. Their role in Rabelais's
novel is immense."[6] Dialect is indispensable to Rabelais's "linguistic
farce," his "linguistic masks": "The dialects become complete images and types of speech and thought" (*Rabelais* 469). Whatever is
Gascon and local, non-existent tongues, idioms, jargons, other national languages, macaronic sentences, intonations, parodies of
Latin, are all tossed together in an "intense interanimation and
struggle," which is, among other things, a class struggle and the
birth of a new historical era (*Rabelais* 468–71). Bakhtin concludes,
in sentences that apply to Scots and Caribbean-London writing although these writers are not as heteroglot as Rabelais and Shakespeare on the edge of Renaissance consciousness: "another
language means another philosophy and another culture but in
their concrete and not full translatable form. The exceptional freedom and pitiless gaiety of the Rabelaisian image were possible only
on the confines of languages" (*Rabelais* 472–73).

In connecting Bakhtin's ideas on social heteroglossia to the centrifugal and entropic energies of dialect writing, I find elucidation
in writers who come after and go beyond Bakhtin. Roland Barthes's
1973 essay on "The Division of Languages" proposes a study of sociolects, social languages like psychoanalytic or Marxist discourse that
separate any culture by clan, class, or profession—a study that is
thinkable only with a founding act of evaluation whereby we distin-

guish discourses *within power* from discourses *outside power.*[7] Gilles Deleuze and Félix Guattari read Kafka as exemplar of a minor
literature, but for them minor is not a term of disparagement: a
minor literature "doesn't come from a minor language; it is rather
that which a minority constructs within a major language."[8] Some
Scots writers claim they are writing another language entirely, because Scots itself exists as a grouping of dialectal subsets; aside from
linguistic reasons for doubting this, the sociopolitical case for taking
Scots and other discourses as dialects of English is well worth making with the help of Deleuze and Guattari. Among the characteristics of a minor literature in their definition: a high coefficient of
deterritorialization, such as that of the German and Jewish culture
within Kafka's Prague; everything in minor literatures is political;
and everything takes on a "collective value" (Deleuze and Guattari
16–17). Deleuze and Guattari mean what they say about collective
politics, and they take this kind of writing as revolutionary within the
major language, but they argue against the kind of single sense
which comes to dominate a unified national language, as well as
against the very "subject of the enunciation . . . [and the] subject of
the statement": "Since articulated sound was a deterritorialized
noise but one that will be reterritorialized in sense, it is now [in
minor literature] sound itself that will be deterritorialized irrevoca-
bly, absolutely" (21).

How can sound as sound overthrow, or at least partly disestablish
a dominant discourse of sense, particularly in dialect writers who are
not as experimental as Kafka? Authors of recent studies of cognition
in art argue, to me persuasively, that nonunderstanding sets in motion a furious search behavior: what would it mean to claim that this
behavior had political meanings, too? How far in my two examples
can this nonunderstanding of the language of the other, where glim-
mers of English sense and syntax shine through, dis-place the one
who hears it aloud or in the mind?

The distinctive rhythms of my two example poems, one a high-
modernist laconicism and the other based on musical rhyme and
refrain, both alert to current practice in free verse, give evidence
that the social, whether it be border culture or diaspora culture,
penetrates in poetry down to the level of form. I want to address
the issue of rhythmic phrasing and intonation with these examples
because Bakhtin's views on the issue are rarely discussed and never,
to my knowledge, contested. Most often Bakhtin uses *rhythm* and *in-*

2: BAKHTIN AND THE SOCIAL POETICS OF DIALECT

tonation as analytical terms that help us to explain the relation of author and hero in the novel.[9] The terms refer to close-to-the-text segmentations of a novel's dialogic content, specific smaller and larger enactments of Bakhtin's version of meaning, namely meaning held between two consciousnesses, held in common and struggled for. Bakhtin is explicitly opposed to the way of the Formalists, who take rhythm in a single consciousness and describe how devices in the work of art activate the reader's cognition. For Bakhtin, however, rhythm in poetry would appear to be of a different *intentionality* from that in the novel because this rhythm is a subatomic, sound-and-structure level expression of the monologism of poetic style. Fiction's mode of intentionality is the highest and most dialogic kind, "a free image of another's language which expresses not only a stylized but also a stylizing language- and art-intention" ("Discourse" 362).[10] Against this, I propose to show that poetry has a claim upon social intentionality that is other but equal. Poetry too, notably dialect poetry, gives the image of a language as the image of a culture, or one living strand in the weave of a culture.

SOCIAL HETEROGLOSSIA IN THE UNITED KINGDOM IN THE THATCHER ERA

There is space only to gesture at the historical narrative of focal events in the United Kingdom that might make a *chronotope* of the period since 1939, if we can use Bakhtin's term to apply to historical as well as fictional time. Certain rhyming events take on allegorical significance: World War II and the Falklands and Persian Gulf Wars and the national consciousness raised therein, Suez in the 1950s and the Gulf in the 1990s, crises over the possession of oil, adventures of the first world against and within the third, labor economic u-turns, overall rise in social equality in the postwar years until Margaret Thatcher's ascendancy in 1979, and decline since. A major survey of the history and culture of post-1945 Britain, Bryan Appleyard's *The Pleasures of Peace*, rightly puts the word "peace" into its title, for the lack of an all-encompassing war is itself a characterizing feature for period synthesis.[11] But the peace has not been benign. Hugh Seton-Watson's judgment may stand for others: "In 1976, the United Kingdom was not united, and Great Britain was no longer great, due to the actions not of its enemies but of its own citizens."[12] That was written in the mid 1970s, when North Sea oil was beginning to come in off Aberdeen as a respite to the economic plunge—but also bringing with it wishes for greater autonomy in Scotland, and offering no way out of the Northern Irish questions, still violent, still unsolved as a drain on resources and good will. In 1976, the top 1 percent of citizens owned more than the bottom 80 percent.[13] Modest gains in multiculturalism, even into the Thatcher years, have not counterbalanced the losses on so many fronts. Is there a chronotope image for industrial decline, loss of nerve nationally and internationally, high unemployment, diminution of civic cohesiveness, Europhobia and Tunnelphobia? No single physical image, no selective plotting of focal events, could be complex enough.

It is essential to take this account down into the discourse and counterdiscourse of the period. This era's central problems, for the historian of "Britain's unique mixture of adversary politics and a corporate bias,"[14] are those of class and empire: struggles over welfare state, education and medicine, trades-union roles and the place of strikes and slowdowns; and struggles over the rightness of divesting empire, and then over the immigration that resulted from giving it back and away, with major marking points the Enoch Powell speech demanding Black and Asian repatriation (1968) and the city disturbances, which British Blacks do not themselves call riots, in the 1970s and 1980s. One source for dialect writing is the Black British section in *New British Poetry* (1988), where Fred D'Aguilar in his introduction defines his poets "by residence rather than by possession of a passport" and argues the work he has chosen is one version of British poetry as a whole in the 1980s.[15] Until the 1960s, E. J. Hobsbawm affirms in *Nations and Nationalities Since 1780*, "'Britishness' in terms of law and administration, was a simple matter of being born to British parents on British soil, marrying a British citizen, or being naturalized. It is a far from simple matter today [1990]."[16] It has become far from simple in the matter of discourse and intonation as well.

There is a dominant discourse of nation as Queen and Church, class as unwritten punctillios of deference, memory as heritage, nature as humanized pastoral landscape. Elaborating the dominant are the leading tendencies in the university disciplines, for example belletristic analytical literary study, empiricist history, language philosophy with a horror of continental speculation, avoidance of sociological disciplines until recently, the refusal to teach advanced management science because it makes too much of dirty-handed trade—and in the past decade, profound cuts to all higher education, aimed at eliminating faculty. And yet under the fiercest free market Tory administration in modern British history there have emerged openings to dispersive, centrifugal energies of discourse: a brilliant left and feminist publishing scene, which is having a commercial success; revisions of traditional disciplines, so that literature is turning into cultural studies and history "from below" is a strong trend, bringing ordinary people back into the story. Part of this direction also, in language study where it is relevant to this paper, is a new social-historical account of dialect, explicitly an attempt to go beyond philology,[17] and a critical attitude toward the use and defense of standard English (Tony Crowley).[18] A more acute and focused consciousness of social heteroglossia, the clash of discourses within the nation that makes the nation itself multiple, is manifested in recent poetry's obsession with the decentered speaking subject (Jeremy Prynne, Ian Sinclair). Scholarship in several fields increasingly in the United Kingdom looks to Mikhail Bakhtin for a description of heterglot struggle, and to Antonio Gramsci and Raymond Williams for ideas on how counterhegemony may be engaged by intellectual workers. Bakhtin in particular gives Anglicists another idea of what literary study and the national questions might be in the postcolonial era, when the excellence of English writing is increasingly in places outside the United Kingdom, and inside is found in names of foreign natives (Buchi Emicheta, Salman Rushdie, Hanif Kureishi).

Within this chronotope, the Scots and Caribbean communities, each with more than one distinct dialect, have their contrastive social being.[19] Scottish culture is border culture constituting its nation within a nation, north of a line, Hadrian's Wall, specifically built to keep the proto-Scottish Picts from advancing south.[20] Scotland gave its own King James VI to the southern nation in the 1603 union of the crowns, and in the Act of Union of 1707 gave over its independence institutions. So the relationship is long, geographic, and fraternal, though never less than prickly, hence perhaps the national image of the thistle. If it once was a colonial connection, during the eighteenth century with its Risings and the nineteenth with its Highland Clearances, it was never colonized to have its people directly exploited but rather to put down and hold down insurrection on land contiguous with England. The Scottish connection is more properly precolonial than colonial.[21] Caribbean culture in England is a recent diaspora culture from the former colonies—English-speaking, slave-keeping, sugar-growing colonies, composed of persons who emigrated from the margins to the metropolitan center in the post-colonial period, most of them after 1948. The diaspora culture, by contrast with the border culture, is one of displacement and transplantation, bringing other modes of thinking and living into the capitalist, technocratic monoculture of London, Birmingham, and Liverpool. There is no crossing of a physically proximate border, no land of origin to which people return, for usually there is no going back.

In Hugh MacDiarmid and certain other Scottish writers such as leftist playwright John McGrath, there is a staged contempt for English, both language and people. They treasure their difference, no place more eloquently than in the dialect, but even in the mid 1970s at the heady moment of Scottish oil revenues and the Scottish National Party with its thoughts of splitting off or at least of devolution, this was not a revolutionary consciousness, and the tone is one of strenuous dissent within the national family. For unmasked revolutionary thinking as part of the mix of many other kinds of discourse, diaspora Caribbean and Asian people (who have suffered discrimination in housing and schooling, and trouble with the police) seem to have a better fit with the Deleuze-Guattari requirement of being political and collective *in everything*. Between Scots and Carribean dialect writing, the social soil and the literary tone are markedly different, even in respect of the Caribbean poetry's being a bardic recitative performance writing with far greater closeness to the forms and rhythms of music: the intergenre of an interculture.

Tom Leonard is an urban writer—in the Robert Burns-Hugh Mac-Diarmid dialect tradition, which avoids pastoral themes and rhyme-and-meter forms—angry at the relegation of Scotland. But not Scotland in the wee-kailyard-thistle-kilts-Harry Lauder nostalgia—rather a Scotland in touch with something beyond its debased heritage and beyond England:

> aw theez sporran heads
> tahty scoan vibes
> thi haggis trip
> bad buzz man
> dead seen

goahty learn new langwij
sumhm ihnturnashnl
Noah Glasgow hangup[22]

Leonard is willing to be rude. The protagonist speakers of his poems are working men on the streets, prejudices and all, rejecting their standard-English educations, the homogenizing of the London-based media, feminism, university culture with its pretensions. Leonard's short free-verse line, learned, he has stated, from William Carlos Williams, packs violent social energies in delicate short spaces.[23] His most quoted and anthologized poem, "Unrelated Incident (3)," has never been analyzed from the perspective of double-voicing. Free-verse lineation, the main inheritance from Williams's modernism, permits him to gain expressive form without metaphors and similes (except for the lapsed metaphors of "scruff" and "belt-up"), without rhyme and meter. The dominant of style is laconicism: sentences from two to ten words, none of the sentences coincident with a line, giving a lurching feeling with emphasis typically on one key term per line, repeated words such as "talk," truth," "right." Another lack of coincidence is between English words and the orthography of this Scots: usually two into one as in "wanna" and "canny." In prosody as in lexis, issues of segmentation are foregrounded. But of course the major joke of segmentation is more global, because the official voice of the BBC announcer has been colonized by the street voice of the Glasgow scruff, who makes explicit the social meanings of state and authority, including coercive meanings like the final "belt up." But a working class speaker *telling himself* to shut up exposes the pretension of authority and shows himself not subject to it. Within the poem the connection between speaking good English and speaking the truth is mockingly detached, thus opening a space for the nonstandard speaker to have his own truth.

Two meanings and two voices inhabit the same orthography in the poem—or really slightly different orthographies, since "thi-the" and "talk-tok" are used differentially but not in any order that would show one or the other speaker and culture winning out or finally becoming pure, uninfluenced. The very point of the text is their inseparability, yet within that the division and clash of discourses. The official speaker is known by parodied attitudes and salutation; the other is know by his dialect. The establishment announcer, a focal figure in the culture as controller and definer, is himself controlled. There could not be a more perfect example of a text internally dialogized. This is proof that double-voicing exists in poetry as a mode, so the analysis sets Bakhtin against Bakhtin's own dismissal of poetry as monologic. This is a small but theoretically explosive example, rather similar to the storytelling voice of Smith the teenage thief in Alan Sillitoe's "Loneliness of the Long Distance Runner" (1959), showing by doing that working class speakers need not be consigned to restricted logical and linguistic codes.[24]

To turn from border to diaspora: in the West Indies, unlike India or Ceylon, English is the central majority language. Under colonial rule, there was from the start a cleavage in island dialect-speaking workers. Chattel slavery was abolished in 1838, but racism did not disappear for a century and more after that, as C. L. R. James's wonderful cultural history of West Indian cricket, *Beyond a Boundary*, demonstrates for the decades of the 1920s to the 1950s.[25] With the growth of island nationalism after World War II, a few dialect novels were written, and Jamaica produced a lively dialect poet in Louise Bennett, whose narratives and satires in ballad form were influential on writers who emigrated to England in the 1950s and 1960s.[26]

There was a more massive influence, though: the 1960s meant the arrival on the world scene of West Indian music, with the popularity of reggae and the dub poetry of disc jockeys turned singers. The intertwining of nationalism, reggae music, and Rastafarian belief carried island life, politics, and rhythm into the middle of a vast international youth culture. With these also went, through recorded lyrics, the dialects that dispense with past and future tenses and possess their own modes of pluralization and negation. In 1976, as a poet with two published books, Linton Kwesi Johnson wrote an essay on "Jamaican Rebel Music" to show the social and spiritual roots in slavery of the music of Bob Marley, U Roy, and others. Reggae, dub, and ska music, with black and two-tone recording groups, are not just sidelight or soundtrack or sociological oddity, for even while partly co-opted and commercialized, this music is central to West Indian cultural opposition.

The music is crucial as a practice and a symbol precisely because it crosses over into interculture so easily. Blacks were forced to become a diaspora culture by being taken from Africa to the Caribbean, and of course elsewhere too, including England. When they came voluntarily to England during and after World War II, as

Crown Colony members, they found that Britons "weren't expecting us," to quote one Jamaican.[27] About 495,000 people of West Indian origin now live in the United Kingdom, making 1 percent of the population of fifty-five million. This is not the place to tell the story of the racism they met, Enoch Powell's "rivers of blood" speech, attempts at repatriation, civic disturbances, or achievements in finding a sense of being and belonging. Peter Fryer, Paul B. Rich, and Paul Gilroy have well covered that, and Gilroy in particular has discussed the role of music in creating an interpretive community: as one of the cultural and political practices enabling British blacks generally to step "outside the confines of modernity's most impressive achievement—the nation state."[28] Gilroy insists on retaining *race* as an analytic category, "not because it corresponds to any biological or epistemological absolutes, but because it refers investigation to the power that collective identities acquire by means of their roots in tradition. These identities, in the forms of white racism and black resistance, are the most volatile political forces in Britain today" (Gilroy 247). The resistance is sometimes a humorous challenge to standard language. There are other forms and types, including a wide variety of women's writing in standard and dialect, which work through the issue of what to confront first, white racism or black male sexism.[29]

Kwesi Johnson's "It dread inna Inglan" is read to musical accompaniment; it is not, or not obviously, dialogical. The poem is only partial when read off the page; its full realization is recorded with the author's voice speaking over a reggae beat with a background of occasional crowd chants of "Free George Lindo!" In the recording, Kwesi Johnson repeats the whole poem twice, and except for the protest politics of this, the whole thing sounds like a *sprechgesang* in the midst of a wild party. If this is dialogue at all, it is a dialogue of voices in basic agreement: of text with itself in repetition of the whole on the recording, of Kwesi Johnson's voice with the reggae beat and the echo from the crowd, of statement and refrain every stanza, of different people of color—West Indian, African, Asian. Still, one doubts whether Bakhtin would consider the poem dialogic in his stronger sense: very likely, this is the kind of poem he would set against the internally dialogized novel, in his privileging of narrative.

Kwesi Johnson names names and places, names racism, argues with *but-kaw-far* reason-giving phrasing, and ends the whole with two

direct statements of deduction and call for action. There is a deterri-
torializing gesture in the title-term "dread," which carries a rich
cargo of Rastafarian meaning. According to Gordon Roelehr, dread
is the quality in the face of Hailie Selassie and of the lion, dread is
"fierce energy, resolve and an underlying sense of the tragic . . . that
quality which defines the static fear-bound relationship between the
'have-gots' and the 'have-nots' . . . the historic tension between the
slaver and the slave, between the cruel ineptitude of power . . . and
introspective menace and the dream of Apocalypse on the part of
the down-trodden."[30] Dread has migrated with its scenario of fear
and politics from Kingston, Jamaica, to London, England. But there
is also reterritorialization: "we are here to stay / inna Inglan / inna
disya time yah." With a poem of this sort, one remembers Kwesi
Johnson's emphasis on Jamaican religious traditions from his essay
on reggae, and also Cornel West's remarks on black culture and
postmodernism, where West speaks of "kinetic orality, passionate
physicality and combative spirituality" as the weapons of black religious ideological response to America imaged as oppressive Egypt.[31]
For there are rhetorical styles that form communities, not only the
subversive joy and historical patience of religion in West Indies culture, but also, as here, "antiphonal styles and linguistic innovations
that accent fluid, improvisational identities . . . syncopations and
polyrhythms that assert one's somebodiness in a society in which
one's body has no public worth, only economic value as a laboring
mechanism" (West 93). It may well be that we need to study dialogue in the culture and art of community formation, where the
idea of struggle of languages has meanings Bakhtin has not ex-
plored. In resistance communities, within the affinity group lack of
struggle could be a preeminent value. In those communities, the art
would be different, avoiding highly finished, heavily labored effects—avoiding irony, fending off the voices and registers of dominant discourse as unworthy dialogic partners.

In this respect, and based on these examples, though both are dialect poets coming from minority sites within English and the United
Kingdom, Kwesi Johnson is a different kind of writer from Leonard.
Leonard has a high-art avant-garde measure and sound-look, with
the jagged rhythms of international modernism. Leonard more
than Kwesi Johnson suits Bakhtin's point about stages of lyric in an
early philosophical essay, "Author and Hero in Aesthetic Activity,"
namely that a voice may break or fail: in realistic or cynical lyric, as

in Heine, Baudelaire, Annensky, the voice steps outside the chorus (170–71). Musically, prosodically, Kwesi Johnson with his more kinetic orality, his refrains and collective first person plural has not, or not fully, stepped forward out of the chorus. We found a fissure down the middle of each word in Leonard, but nothing of the sort in Kwesi Johnson. This is the difference between the immemorial border culture and the upstart diaspora culture, both jostling within the "process teeming with future and former languages"[32] that is English.

Afterword 2002

This is the earliest essay in the book, dating from 1991, and shows its origins not only by references to the English-Only proposed amendment (failed and forgotten in the U.S.) and to the Thatcher era in the U.K.—but also by being a typical first effort in a method, an enthusiastic use of part of a theoretical frame to illuminate a small body of writing. The two poems that I take for examples here are responses to dominant English languages of their day; so my own historical references to the Thatcher period have not entirely lost their pertinence, as social moorings for those poems. My synthesis from many mentions and hints of Bakhtin's idea of dialect, under the heading of heteroglossia, is perhaps the best contribution of this piece, but there is no recursive criticism of Bakhtin's theoretical frame. I was later to find parallel, Bakhtin-conscious 1990s efforts on Scots dialect by Roderick Watson (Stirling) and Robert Crawford (St. Andrews), and another Scottish scholar, Alastair Renfrew (Strathclyde, Glasgow), took a dialogic page in an essay to reply to something here.

Work toward and beyond this article led me to the field of Scottish Studies, and to wide reading in Burns, MacDiarmid, Sidney Goodsir Smith, Robert Garioch, and other dialect and also Gaelic- and English-language writers. From there I went on to historical studies, concerning an anomalous corner of Europe that is a nation without a state, though after 1997 Scotland had its own devolved Parliament. I now teach one of the few courses in modern Scottish literature west of the Rockies, and I have published on "The Matter of Scotland," on Burns and moral philosophy, and on monologism in recent Scottish fiction.

For a year in the mid 1990s I made plans to write a book about poetries in dialects of English: the Scots of Robert Burns and Hugh MacDiarmid, the Dorset of William Barnes, Lincolnshire in Alfred Tennyson, Jamaican in Jean Binta Breeze and others, St. Lucian in Derek Walcott, and Afro-American in Sherley Anne Williams and others. It seemed important to consider the role of orthography— spelling styles and conventions, and their relation to speech-patterns as sounded out—as influencing the actual reading of dialect verse. All these writers are able to write in standard English, and they sometimes do, and the code switching gives them greater flexibility of tone and subject matter than writers who only possess standard. On the other hand, it is my observation that particularly with Burns, Barnes, and MacDiarmid, poems in dialect have greater moral force and more interesting sounds—their English poems have bland platitudes, and their dialect poems have the intense outlines of newly minted language, though both come from what is plainly the same sensibility and may even be on very similar themes. How can this be? And what does it mean to say this, as a judgment from a standard speaker who prefers dialect on aesthetic and social grounds? To answer would explain further the social poetics of dialect writing, as supplication and as peremptory challenge to a standard-speaking reader. But I decided not to write this out because I judged there is no sufficient audience either for dialect poetry or for its defense; ironically, since the time of Burns, the social poetics of dialect has been self-limiting and prevents further utterance about this kind of utterance.

3

"Easier to Die than to Remember":
Inner Speech in Basil Bunting

WHEN YOU PUT ON EARPHONES AND LISTEN TO THE TAPE OF BASIL BUN-
ting reading *Briggflatts,* hearing him in the back of your head as you
follow him on the page with your eyes, his Northern speech becomes
for a time your own inner speech.[1] You enter a dialect and an
ideolect, and they enter you. Hearing the long poem in Bunting's
voice brought forward, at least for me, one passage near the end of
part 4. Merely reading, I had never noticed it as a center of feeling.
After a dense furious page on Aneurin and Taleisin and owls and
men as killers, the longest lines in the poem, he changes to eight
luminous lines on the music of Domenico Scarlatti, and then he
turns on his own tape of a Scarlatti sonata and speaks over it an
erotic alba, old man telling of a young man's dawn:

> My love is young but wise. Oak, applewood,
> her fire is banked with ashes till day.
> The fells reek of her hearth's scent,
> her girdle is greased with lard;
> hunger is stayed on her settle, lust in her bed.
> Light as a spider floss her hair on my cheek which a puff scatters,
> light as a moth her fingers on my thigh.
> We have eaten and loved and the sun is up,
> we have only to sing before parting:
> Goodbye, dear love.
>
> Her scones are greased with the fat of fried bacon,
> her blanket comforts my belly like the south.
> We have eaten and loved and the sun is up.
> Goodbye.

(CP 67)

The timbre of Bunting's voice made me believe that there is a memory-overlay, in this present tense, of the speaker in his sixties and the lad in his teens before World War I, the lad he was; and an overlay of addressees—both the girl of long ago and the reader who senses the poem is closing. Bunting may also be saying "Goodbye" to himself, his talent. In fact, these lines carry the primary image of virtue and well-being in the poem, yet they are edged with elegy; also with quirky humor in that verb "reek" and in the way the Northern word "girdle" can convey the linkage of loving and eating, because Bunting's note says the Northern word for "griddle" is "girdle" (*CP* 171). He is smiling as he reads "Her girdle is greased with lard," yet even here he is insisting that the Northern word contains the double meaning, indeed more meaning than the standard word.

Many images from this passage in part 4 take us back to the love scene in part 1 and ahead to the ending in part 5, where the speaker concludes: "She has been with me fifty years" (*CP*, 72). Bunting spoke of *Briggflatts* as "an Autobiography, but not a record of fact." Still, as his genre marker at the head of the long poem he wrote "An Autobiography." To me it does not matter if the plot of "love murdered," in his words (*CP* 54), is a record of fact or not, since this is the plot of the poem as Bunting wrote it out in sequence. It is enough to make a poem of over seven hundred lines, but not a novelist's plot because it omits motivation for the murdering of love and it omits the middle: What are the events of those fifty years? At the end of part 5, the speaker twice claims that then is now. What cannot be shown is declared. No atonement, but continuing love and shame have been declared in the light of day.

There is a beautiful trope of reluctance-to-declare in part 1 when Bunting says:

> No hope of going back.
> Hounds falter and stray,
> shame deflects the pen.
> Love murdered neither bleeds nor stifles
> but jogs the draftsman's elbow.
> What can he, changed, tell
> her, changed, perhaps dead?
> Delight dwindles. Blame
> stays the same.

(*CP* 54)

"Love murdered" is now a memory effect and a writing effect. Language will not touch it, but language is all Bunting has. "Delight dwindles," but we have already seen, in "My love is young but wise," that memory and writing have some kind of power because that lyric moment is a rehearsal of deep delight. We are now able, perhaps, to say what happened in those fifty years dropped from the plot of the poem. *Bunting's poems happened.* His writings are all one way or another related to the originary trauma of love murdered. Having *Briggflatts* as the crown of Bunting's odes, sonatas, and translations, and his last major work, requires from us a reassessment of his two linked and dominating themes of breakable love and cut-out-of-stone literary art. Because he left on the morning when "We have eaten and loved and the sun is up," he entered a writing life, to quote his preface to *Collected Poems,* "here and there now and then over forty years and four continents" (*CP* 11). He entered a life of sexual longing and inconstancy, wartime wandering, rotten jobs at a newspaper rewrite desk, all of which he summed up in part 5 as running in a boat in a hurricane when "the star you steer by is gone" (*CP* 71). However, had he stayed true to a love who was young but wise, his life would have been a single night or season, full of the usual events, but not, it may be, of writing.

Without *Briggflatts* we might not have noticed Bunting's meditation on writing and memory, a continuing inquiry in his work that makes him, from 1925 and the poem "Villon" onwards, a poet highly sophisticated in the methods of representing inner speech. "It is easier to die than to remember," he wrote (*CP* 55). Pursuing to the fullest that one line of *Briggflatts* might enable a reading, if partial, of the long poem and whole of Bunting. Our century's most punishing poet of vanquished difficulty, Bunting finds it preferable to die than to face the shame. Better loss of self than murder of love. He insists that those are the stakes. Morally, it could even be worse: willed amnesia; part 2 has the line, "to humiliate love, remember / nothing" (*CP* 58). Dying and remembering have this in common with inner speech. Nobody can conduct an interior dialogue, or remember back fifty years, or die *for us.* We own these actions, and since in some measure we are they, any theft or breakdown, such as Alzheimer's, is terrible to imagine.

This man famous for Northern local knowledge and for close descriptive attention to animals and birds is just as often attentive to mental states, memory work, the cognitive roots and stirrings of discourse. In this he is like one of his great Northern masters, William Wordsworth. I have found that to get to the ways Bunting is a social poet, one has to work through his interiority, his memory writing, his sense of history. I began with the idea of interpreting Bunting as a modernist Northern instance of the clash of political discourse in United Kingdom poetry since World War II. I do have something to say, near the end, about the cultural politics of nation, newspaper language, and masculine desire. But still, I should say that my original hypothesis failed. Bunting said he was not a political or didactic poet, and he was not. For myself, I do not mean to argue that lyric poetry has no relation to society; rather that the mediations are winding and attenuated, and that one way to trace some of their turns in Bunting is to follow up the linkages and estimate the proportions between outer and inner speech.

Enter Mikhail Bakhtin. The Russian philosopher of communication is best known in the West for his accounts of social locations of speaking—"social heteroglossia" in the Michael Holquist translation. Bakhtin studies the voices of class and profession that come into literary and other works, and the way these "sociolects" are in endless dialogue. For him dialogue is a contest at the borders of two consciousnesses, not a cozy sharing of horizons. While never losing sight of the social text, for texts are always social in Mikhail Bakhtin, I want first to honor the actual center of Bunting's work by collating Bakhtin's lesser-known, scattered remarks on inner speech, and using those remarks to focus on Basil Bunting's speech acts and speech genres, and his habits of meditation and memory. I propose to read Bunting against Bakhtin, primarily to deliver a different Bunting from the one we know in current studies and in Bunting's own interviews and literary opinions.

Born in 1895 and 1900, Bakhtin and Bunting were contemporaries, and each in his separate culture experienced two world wars, exile, and neglect, and a miraculous late recognition brought about by admirers. For all their differences of training and of the angle of entry into literature, they shared a concern for the social dynamics of dialect writing and of spoken intonation generally. They despised abstract consciousness in all its forms, but religion was not for them an abstraction. Russian Orthodox Christianity is the first cause of everything in Bakhtin's thought, and a kind of skeptical Quakerism that thinks Hume and God in the same thought is where Bunting arrives from *Briggflatts* until his death in 1985. Which of the two wrote this?

> Take a dialogue and remove the voices . . . remove the intonations (emotional and individuating ones), carve out abstract concepts and judgments from living words and responses, cram everything into one abstract consciousness—and that's how you get dialectics.[2]

It is from Bakhtin; but it could easily be a bit of fireworks in a letter from Bunting to Louis Zukofsky. Bunting's bitter reproaches against critics, professors, and readers with psychological theories probably derive as much from this principled hatred of abstraction as from a wish to shepherd the image of his work.

In the preface to her 1991 book on Bunting, Victoria Forde states that there is "no need to *theorize* about poetry, which Bunting disparaged, but simply recognize the art of his craftsmanship."[3] Peter Makin uses a whole final chapter to struggle against what he calls post-Lacanian critics, so he does confront but only to declare theory largely irrelevant to the shaping of Bunting's verse.[4] Forde and Makin adhere, I submit, too closely to Bunting's intuitive bias. Makin is astute to see that his own traditional method of relating theme and style is undercut by the skepticisms of current literary theory, and he is able to score some points against theory as he defends and illustrates the art of a modernist poet. In the best book we are likely to have on Bunting for some years, it is fascinating to see the Bunting-Makin commonsense, phenomenal habit of mind at war with the anti-intuitive, linguistic bias of contemporary literary theory. Makin is eloquently dialogic whenever he takes up Bunting's poetry, and only soberly dialectic when he gets to theorists like Stanley Fish in his final chapter.

Just because interpretation is dependent upon textual and rhetorical procedures, interpretation need not be subjective, as Peter Makin fears. Bakhtin's is one method that, seeking an open unity in the work, in the culture the work represents, avoids relativism and also avoids dogmatism. This is an account of human behavior and an attitude toward utterances, not a set of practices. So it is hard to figure out how to crank down the level of generality and make dialogism work as a specific, useful reading. A dialogic reading accepts all the evidences and many of the opinions of books like Makin's, but gives another view of the evidence. Dialogism, which should never be taken for *conversation*, starts with the distinction between self and other as central, and groups beneath it other dyads: inner/outer, monologic/dialogic, unofficial/official. Unlike most philosophies and criticisms, it makes a complete account of human behavior based on *addressivity*, the immense and delicate adjustments people make to each other as they communicate. The other person is necessary, and even in inner speech is inescapable. Taken with full seriousness, this must mean the abandonment, or rather subsumption, of nearly all Western rational metaphysics since Descartes—and also, for example, of Romantic organicist or biographical poetics, and of Russian Formalism's and American New Criticism's pursuit of the device, like meter or rhyme, as the only hero of literature.

For Bakhtin, outsidedness, *vnenakhodimost'*, is the hero. "The word in language is half someone else's," he wrote in a famous passage in "Discourse in the Novel": "It becomes 'one's own' only when the speaker populates it with his own intention, his own accent."[5] *Word* in Russian, *slovo*, can and in Bakhtin does have the widest possible meaning as *discourse*. Bakhtin's method exceeds linguistics and stylistics, because it refuses to isolate bits of language, words removed from dialogue, expunged from speech-life: "But I hear voices in everything and dialogic relations among them," he wrote late in life.[6] Dialogue is shared differences, nonharmonious wholes; so too with *carnival* and *novel*, other terms in Bakhtin's system describing simultaneously interacting differences. Outsidedness is the defining condition governing the perception of persons, languages, whole societies. We can never see ourselves as finished; we can only see others that way. The self never has full self-presence, and this enables us to receive the gift of insight that outsidedness brings when we are aware of gaps, impossibilities. This is not a Romantic longing for wholeness, but a celebration of outsidedness, because only from the other can one get oneself, get categories for fixing the self.[7] Thus with Bunting: when he was a lad, so *Briggflatts* has it, he was able to receive himself from a girl, and hence much was owed to her and much betrayed. Admitting this in the poem completed a pattern and there was not a great deal more to write. All this is speculation, and yet I find some support in the fragment we have from his last attempt at a sonata, three stanzas on love and death that he produced on seeing a beautiful adolescent girl on the moonlit deck of a boat: starting again in his eighties with another who was young but wise.[8]

Inner speech is inseparable from outer speech, and both go by the general, dialogic rules of all human behavior. I have chosen to emphasize inner speech, though Bakhtin does not, because I believe Basil Bunting used his work to a large degree to explore mental life. If we go by proportions alone, Bunting devoted more effort to this than Bakhtin. Across the whole career, I have counted seventeen crucial passages that explicitly discuss or provide analogies for inner speech, including these four from different poems and eras in the career:

> ... the gracious music
> Thoughts make moving about
>
> (*UP* 9)

> Circe excellent utterer of her mind
>
> (*CP* 17)

> What we think in private
> will be said in public
>
> (*CP* 47)

> we have heard
> voices speech eludes allude to
>
> (*CP* 112)

Also there is the magnificent number 15 in book 1 of the Odes, which is a full treatment of how, to quote, "thought's intricate polyphonic score dovetails with the tread / sensuous things / keep in our consciousness"—wittily Buntingesque in the ending exaggeration that likens death to deafness to accent, which for a poet it would be (*CP* 101).

Bakhtin's sparse comments on inner speech are philosophically rich and entirely consonant with the rest of his thought on dialogism. Papers and books from the Bakhtin Circle, by his friends Valentin Voloshinov and Pavel Medvedev, or by Bakhtin and given for publication under their names, do significantly expand the reach of the topic of interior discourse.[9] Also we have the remarkable work, convergent but it seems unknown to Bakhtin, of Russian psychologist Lev Vygotsky, whose speculative and empirical accounts on inner speech have been developed in Russian psycholinguistics since the time of Vygotsky's death in the mid thirties.[10] I rely heavily on Bakhtinian scholars who have discussed the role of inner speech, especially Caryl Emerson.[11] For my purposes here, I am going to keep these other names behind and under the name of Bakhtin, except for just two context-building comments from Caryl Emerson and George Steiner. In her essay on "The Outer Word and Inner Speech," Emerson remarks that "An awareness of the gap between inner speech and outer might function . . . as an index of individual consciousness, as a measure of our escape from fixed plots and roles, as a prerequisite for discourse itself."[12] George Steiner's essay, "The Distribution of Discourse," takes as its mission what Lev Vygotsky proposed at the end of his book in the thirties, namely the formulation of a "historical theory of inner speech." Steiner finds that "the shift in the balance of discourse since the seventeenth century has been outward," and that in consequence "we have lost a considerable measure of control over the fertile ground of silence."[13] This special silence, the control of inner speech, seems to have become a leading thought for Bunting toward the end of his career, and I will return to it at the end of this essay.

Mikhail Bakhtin was dialogic to the furthest possible extent: he wrote books and gave them to friends to publish under their names. In one of these books of the late twenties, Bakhtin or/as Pavel Medvedev says, "Even inner speech is social . . . oriented toward a possible audience, toward a possible answer":[14] this is my overall point with Bunting. In the same book is the claim that "only the utterance can be beautiful [and] true," which has direct implication now for our practice as readers. It means that the traditional markers of literariness are now largely neglected, or just assumed, as we listen for utterances. The utterance is a unit of communication, a response-unit, responding to others without and others within, and hence the utterance is Bakhtin's hero. The sentence is a unit of language, and the rhyme pair or metrical foot is a further overdetermined unit of language, still more distant from living speech acts; so these cannot really help. The hard part about hearing with some strictness our units of communication is that we live with them and in them so closely. Often we cannot experience them analytically; they are too automatic.

Whether the speech is inner or outer, it seems sensible to say that a Bakhtinian reading will set out to determine the boundaries of each concrete utterance, and will track changes in speaking subjects. In Bakhtin's own books on Rabelais and Dostoevsky, his moves as a reader may seem strange: we get no description of a whole novel, but we get tremendous sensitivity to shifts in speaking subjects, and to boundaries between characters' fields of vision. Without question, elements of value will be left behind as we read Bunting's lyrics with their heavy sound patterns. We will have to see if there is a plausible gain in other spheres, such as responsiveness to (what Michael Holquist has called) the social striation of inner speech.[15]

Now that we have Bakhtin's scissors, his distinction between sentences and utterances, it is time to cut sentencing and rhyming loose and take up three inner-speech issues: *minimal articulation, change of speaking subjects*, and *editing*.

In minimal articulation, literature is assimilated back and down to bodily sounds and behaviors. These pre-speech actions are brought in to show something about minds and texts. The *vox confusa*, that ancient rhetoricians thought the voice of animals, is taken purposely into the human *vox articulata* in the poem. In his infamous sly article on "Bunting and the Quonk and Groggle School," Peter Dale was on to something about Bunting's clotted density in the use of sound, but what he saw as a preference for sound over meaning, finding license in Bunting's own statements, can be understood as a use of chosen effects to convey otherwise unreachable meanings, often ironic.[16] "Tweet, tweet, twaddle, / Tweet, tweet, twat," "Way-O, Bully boys blow! / The Gadarene Swihine have got us in tow," "Stuck, stick, Styx. Styx, eternal, a dwelling": all of the separate sardonic sounds are in "The Well of Lycopolis," and also another type, the final lines on the minimal sound of sighing:

> muttering inaudible beneath the quagmire,
> irresolute, barren, dependant, this page
> ripped from Love's ledger and Poetry's:
> and besides I want you to know for certain
> there are people under the water. They are sighing.
> The surface bubbles and boils with their sighs.
> Look where you will see it.
> The surface sparkles and dances with their sighs
> as though Styx were silvered by a wind from Heaven.
>
> (*CP* 35)

In this kind of effect, pre-speech pulsions, often in rhyme paradigm, are examples of breakdown, pathology, the inability to keep a healthy commerce between inner and outer speech; hence the mocking tone. There are many related instances: eruptions of other languages and scripts, bizarre, unsettling—"Schrecklich," in "Aus dem zweiten Reich," and "Adsunt omnes, omnes et / Villon. / Villon?" in "Villon"; "Yan tan tethera pethera pimp" to begin the "Dentdale Conversation" in pretend dialect; or the playful imagining of a Cattish language with its own rhyming ideograms in "The Pious Cat," Bunting's translation from Obaid-e Zakani. In some of the lyrics, Bunting uses pre-utterance pulsions to judge other persons: in *Briggflatts*, the phonetic compression, jammed up and resisting euphony, brings into *vox articulata* a sound-image of the struggle to know, to face mortality, in other words to judge himself. This is the representation of inner speech trying to become exterior.

If the utterance is the real unit of speech communication, the change of speakers will be the crucial moment in a dialogue. It becomes necessary to find the boundaries of each concrete utterance, to see how the utterance is made final, and to seek its generic form. Bakhtin points to the opening and closing of an utterance as especially volatile; first and last sentence are, he says, on the "front line" of communication, the boundary of change between speaking subjects.[17] Surveying the whole of Bunting, there are very few texts like "The Spoils" that are set up, or partly, as actual dialogue. "Villon," "Chomei at Toyama," and *Briggflatts* are typical in launching a single speaker whose voice then diversifies into other voices, which most often do not listen to the previous one but are arrived at over a gap. Bunting is like most lyric poets in restricting outer dialogue and expatiating on inner dialogue; the polyvocality is that of inner speech. Bakhtin would say: that is why poetry is essentially monologic and monoglossic—but contrasts with the double-voicing of the novel, for which Bakhtin makes extravagant claims. To me it seems poetry is or can be also dialogic, but with a preference for double-voicing within the utterance and not across the boundaries of utterances.

"Villon" and "Chomei" are representations of the totality of the life of isolated speakers at an extreme distance of time and place from Bunting and Bunting's readers. Part translation, part calque or parody, part imaginary incident, part covert Bunting autobiography, these seem much longer than they are because of the severe focus on the inner life, and also because of the quantity of logical gaps being jumped. Villon in prison and Chomei in secluded retirement seem to speak guarded versions of that other trauma Bunting suffered while still a teenager, eighteen months in jail, often in a cell alone, as a conscientious objector during World War I, left literally with his own inner speech and nothing but.

Usually, Bunting is more dialogic as he gestures across the boundaries of utterances. I think of the slowworm's song at the end of part 3 of *Briggflatts*, where a weakened hero, Alexander, is shown listening to this speech from the heart of nature, then getting up refreshed: "So he rose and led home silently through clean woodland / where every bough repeated the slowworm's song" (*CP* 65). In Bunting's world a slowworm, a bough, "A thrush in the syringa" can possess *vox articulata* and enter dialogue with each other and with us. Perhaps half the odes and translations begin with an apostrophe to a woman, a fellow poet, the southwind, Chang Chung, many imagined listeners. "Brag, sweet tenor bull," inaugurating the utterance in *Briggflatts*, is one of the most energetic and delectable openings in any modernist poem, and sets going everything, bull, river, seasons, sex, art. Still, that command to the bull to brag and sing and dance may remind us of the masculinity of Bunting's inner and outer speech: we have utterances to women but they themselves rarely utter. When women get a good long inning of two pages, it is not Peggy Greenbank talking back to Bunting in *Briggflatts*, but Mother Venus in "The Well of Lycopolis" as a drunk cockney drab saying, "Aye, tether me among the maniacs, / it's nicer to rave than reason" (*CP* 30). So far as I can make out, neither of his wives is addressed or mentioned in a single poem. Typically, when poems are addressed to or about other poets, Pound and Eliot always excepted, the fellow writer is *Narciss* or his poems are *versicles*. Bunting's one direct "Envoi to the Reader" imagines that we want to have published his "secret heart," which would be to "Spell out a fart / and have it printed" (*UP* 18). He will show only the selection of inner speech that he has rigorously made. But even after the strictest cancellations, the theme of decay of the body and of life, as the end product of bad thought, bad editing, bad art, resonates everywhere in the writings collected and uncollected. Nowhere is this evident more violently than in the 1965 poem that starts by addressing himself: "You idiot! What makes you think decay will / never stink from your skin?" (*CP* 134).

Bunting's bold openings spring from the conflicts of inner speech. Being able to speak to someone, or to himself, gives him energy, which he can then give away to the addressee. His endings are sometimes more cautious, valedictory, elegiac. The ode that begins "You idiot!" closes on two questions, the most open and tentative form of closure. "The Spoils" also ends on a question mark, and like "Villon" and "The Well of Lycopolis" ends with death by water, graves under water, a somber farewell. The American edition of *Collected Poems* effectively ends, as a book, with Ode 12 of the second book, "Perche no spero," a lyric in three stanzas addressing the body as a cutter riding "free of the sands," "no course to set," ready for the swamping which is death. Bunting had ended that poem in the journal *Agenda* in 1978, "we have . . . / only to drift too long, watch too glumly, and wait, / wait like the proud," but he was right to avoid the cloud-proud rhyme that evoked the heart-stirring simile, and entirely to drop "like the proud" when he collected the poem.[18] That leaves a gap or asymmetry; it wants but does not give the missing rhyme, and it leaves the only one-word line, "wait." as the last line. The ending of the poem and book avoids self-pity.

Often, Bunting's closures have a trope of disavowal, making literal the deletion effect I have just noticed by deleting himself. Bunting's wonderful Horace translation, "Snow's on the fellside, look!"—with its enactive, hand gesture beginning—ends on a self-effacing rhyme: "She won't make much fuss. [Then Bunting makes a double-space gap; long pause and then a parting parenthesis.] (Says Horace, more or less)" (*UP* 46): so the debt to Horace is paid and withdrawn in the same final phrase. He disappears at the end of "The Pious Cat" translation, too, with "I never. It wasn't me, / It was Obaid-e Zakani" (*UP* 55). Far more of Bunting's poems have emphatic, assertive, even ironic endings where the rhyme snaps shut and allusions to endings abound. These poems effectively settle things by telling the reader what to think, as in the reverse logic of "What the Chairman Told Tom," where the businessman-poetry hater exposes his own ignorance. I think the poems where Bunting leaves his utterance vulnerable to reply and even reproach are more productive because they are more tonally subtle.

Briggflatts closes on a Coda with images of an ocean voyage and a slaughtered king, but the poem's plot of love murdered actually ends just above with these lines of aching echoes and aching spaces:

> Finger tips touched and were still
> fifty years ago.

Sirius is too young to remember.
Sirius glows in the wind. Sparks on ripples
mark his line, lures for spent fish.

Fifty years a letter unanswered;
a visit postponed for fifty years.

She has been with me fifty years.

Starlight quivers. I had day enough.
For love uninterrupted night.

(CP 71–72)

In the Warren Tallman-Peter Quartermain interview given in Vancouver in the seventies, Bunting said, "The first line I wrote was the last line of the poem, apart from the Coda."[19] So he wrote "uninterrupted night" before anything else but positioned it last, something to be aimed at and earned by the poem as written. He saved this line because its kernel meaning could not be released before the full presentation of guilt in parts 1 and 2. On the page, next to the "Swiss mountain range" diagram of Briggflatts's structure that he drew for Tallman and Quartermain, he wrote Catullus's line, nox est perpetua una dormienda. Later, breaking into the interview, he insisted that "una dormienda doesn't mean one night, it means a night that is all one, that never varies." I am going to make a daring leap here and claim that, for Bunting, it is easier to die than to remember because first love remembered becomes the meaning of all love. That is, the teenage lad-and-lass night could be seen as a whole life, in imagination, so the various and contingent experiences that came after did not matter.

To end his original initiating utterance gave him a chance to indicate a change of relation to the girl, involving apology and self-acceptance in the new wider framework of the perpetua. But Bunting's word for perpetua is uninterrupted—curiously defensive. On the positive side, when the first thought is withheld to be the last utterance, it sends the writer and reader back to retrace the logic that justifies the final assertion. This gives a longish poem the intensity of lyric throughout. However, dialogically considered, ending on the beginning tends to omit a place for the reader, or addressee generally, to come into the circuit of communication. The speaker is uninterrupted, too, just like the night. There is a tendency to remain in inner speech.

This is a prime piece of editing, very typical of Bunting. Bakhtin says nothing about *editing* as a way in which inner speech is made social. I suspect that some of the best thinking on this topic is being done in the field now known in the United States and United Kingdom as composition theory—scholars who study what student writers, all writers, need to know, at the convergence place of linguistics, cognitive science, education, and literature. Most in that field would, I think, agree with James Moffett that the chief task of writing is "making the implicit appropriately explicit": learning to focus on inner speech, tap off inner speech, and edit the great inner panorama that is us talking to ourselves and hearing voices. It is a process of expatiation, that takes the interplay of inner voices back out into the social world.[20]

Writing is revised inner speech; crucially for Bunting, the mind that passes from inner to outer, and accommodates itself to society, must do so while keeping its integrity. Bunting's was a classical form of modernism that edited out slushy subjectivity by heroic feats of editing. We have seen him editing by re-sequencing the order of his thoughts to make the finale of *Briggflatts*, but far more usual is editing by deletion. "Cut out every word you dare," he told students of writing at Newcastle University.[21] He had earned the right to say this by writing twenty thousand lines for *Briggflatts* and keeping seven hundred, by refusing to keep drafts of poems and mocking those who did, by paring down the *Collected Poems* to the point where it looks slim, but where there is not a single bad poem in the lot, not even a single weak line or extra word. He applied the same standard to others, because late in life as the judge of a competition he could not find one poem out of more than a thousand to approve for an award. And in the early 1930s he ruthlessly slashed through an edition of Shakespeare's Sonnets, dropping redundant or pretty language, sometimes leaving only a line from a sonnet's fourteen.[22] What chutzpah! Whether he was correcting Shakespeare or himself, the rule was always that the poem must seem interactive but *be* edited. Despite his compressions of syntax and his display of throaty Northern sounds, the norm in Bunting is declaratory, conversation-seeming poetry. The writing largely deletes the marks of the effort it took to get written.

Obviously, there will be conflicts between different levels of inner speech, and between inner and outer speech, in any writer. I have focused on inner speech because this notion helps us see something central, characteristic, and perhaps neglected in Bunting; also because no one has ever developed the Bakhtinian theory at length with an example. Now I want to push the analysis to its final term. Briefly, I would sketch just the contours of a social reading that I earlier mentioned might be less congenial for Bunting. That is, precisely because his political ideas were personal he did not think they belonged in a work of verbal art. He edited politics out for the same reason he deleted his prison, World War II, and family experience from a poem he called "An Autobiography." He was unwilling, he said, to "stand emotionally naked."[23] One of Bunting's methods of covering himself, to continue his metaphor, is to employ the outer speech of real or imagined others, what we might define as propositions of subject and what Bakhtin termed social heteroglossia. I refer to the guises called Villon and Chomei, his various translation voices, Cockney and Northumberland dialects, and the miners' speech, parody jingles, and official lingo in the strange 1930 poem, "They say Etna." Rather than pursue these social voices, or search out Bunting's enigmatic politics in works where he seems to be making a commitment, I prefer to attack the general issue with this question: is there a habit of resistance in Bunting where he explicitly sets inner speech against outer word, where he sets the internally persuasive against the authoritative?

The three social discourses that Bunting resists, as these are embodied within himself and the larger culture, are the discourses of *nation, newspaper,* and *masculine desire.*

As for the official discourse of the British nation, Bunting was anti-Southern and pro-Northern in speech pattern, literary politics, choice of place to settle, whisky, sheepdogs, everything. Peter Quartermain's Mountjoy lecture on Bunting as the poet of the North is the definitive account of this side of the work.[24] In the 1940s when Bunting was wing commander, diplomat, reporter, and perhaps spy, he did act as a representative of Englishness; but not one of his poems does that, ever. I think of him as a provincial internationalist, because from his Northern vantage he looks over the top of London for cultural values, to Italy, Persia, and America. If Southern thinking is metropolitan and represents the singleness of the State, for him Northern thinking connects whatever is marginal, local, plural, adulterated, and inconvenient, with the imaginativeness of the global modernist avant-garde.

Bunting's counterdiscourse against newspaper language has its focus in the daring seventy-odd lines about the turd-bakers that open part 3 of *Briggflatts*. The passage is so extreme that all of Bunting's commentators expect Peter Makin to have passed over it in silence or with a shudder of distaste. Treating it in summary and not with full Freudian linkage of anality and the death-instinct, I too am backing away from it, I admit. This is the nadir of *Briggflatts*, and the point in it which most resembles, of all writing I know, the shocking negativity of the Cave of Spleen canto in Pope's *Rape of the Lock*. Reading it over and over, I think we conclude that this is the furthest expression of the most dominant single image cluster in Bunting, a line of logic that leads from dust to excrement to soil to death to personal and artistic oblivion. This is profoundly prevalent in Bunting and needs a full-scale inquiry. I mention it only on my way to the remarkable footnote 26 on Peter Makin's page 147, where Makin tells of receiving two letters from Bunting in 1984–85. The turd-bakers who cry "Sweet shit! Buy!" Bunting explained, "include various who choose baseness, particularly 'the press' (with Hastor for president)"—and the oddly named Hastor turns out to be Hugh Astor of *The Times*. I doubt we would know this without the footnote, but now that we do know, it is possible to relate Bunting's largest constellation of imagery to his covert but violent rejection of the social dirt language of journalism.

The resistance against masculine desire and patriarchal attitudes is harder to see and to argue for, because Basil Bunting is preeminently, stubbornly a writer of every phase of male love and lust. Dozens and dozens of examples are possible, and Sister Victoria Forde may be forgiven if she does not want to go into all that. When I try to read as a feminist, I can well understand and feel sympathetic to the possible discomfort of a woman reader. If we did not have *Briggflatts*, as the crown of the career, very likely the avoidance by Victoria Forde and the likely confrontation-response of a feminist reader would fend off all replies. But in *Briggflatts*, I think Bunting fights through to a critique and understanding of his earlier selves. The poem begins, admittedly, with a sexual romping tenor bull, but it ends with apology, regret, a wider interpretation of love. Along the way it finds a feminine hero, Pasiphae in part 2, who is more crucial to the poem's myth of imaginative courage than Eric Bloodaxe or

Alexander. Bunting had not before stated openly, as he does here, that his speaking subject is an "adult male of a merciless species" (*CP* 66). Above all the poem has those lines I quoted at the very beginning on a girl who is young but wise, lines which show that desire can be mutual and good humored and still be desire. So *Briggflatts*, to the degree that it has Bunting willing to venture into an autobiography where it is easier to die than to remember, is another instance of resisting and modifying an official discourse.

Briggflatts contains, in the senses of holding and managing, the negative energy. To do that, Bunting as the writer had to witness and direct his own inner speech. That would have been quite enough, but he took this text further and set out to be disciple and evangelist of the control of inner speech. This silencing of the mind, what Carlos Castaneda's Mexican Yaqui Indian sorcerer, Don Juan, called the key to spiritual life—namely, "stopping the internal dialogue"—is evident in the Quaker title and the memory-work in the poem.[25] Quakers will testify singly aloud if they wish, but usually they simply sit listening to others or to conscience. (Lisa Kenner says that Bunting, in the summer of his eightieth year at Hugh Kenner's vacation home, would sit in uninterrupted meditation between four and five o'clock every afternoon.[26]) Now, Peter Makin has six exquisite pages on the spirituality of silence in late Bunting (205–10), and to these I would add just the thought that silence is the stilling of inner as well as outer speech. Also let me bring on a final word from Bakhtin, who distinguished between silence and mere absence of sound: "silence," Bakhtin said, "is possible in the human world and *only for a person.*"[27] So silence in the between-time of utterances is also energetic work. It is "ridiculous and lovely," to quote *Briggflatts*; in fact it is exactly right to have this from the Russian philosopher of utterances and from the Northern poet who was a sound-celebrator if ever there was one.

AFTERWORD 2002

This was the Mountjoy lecture at the University of Durham in the spring of 1993. I spent three months at Durham on the invitation of the Basil Bunting Archive at the University Library, and was able to see Bunting landmarks: Lindisfarne island with its Celtic memories, the Quaker meetinghouse at Briggflatts, and the mining towns of

County Durham. Basil Bunting proved to be a reasonable choice for developing Bakhtin's ideas of inner speech through one writer's whole career. Although he hides his relation to inner speech by means of modernist projections and personas, very much in the line of Ezra Pound as Pound's main British disciple, he is always soliciting, always correcting inner speech in his writings. Bunting's range of speaking subjects is wide, as he extends the chronotopes of his writings to ancient Japan and Iran, far from times and places Pound valued; he can also, in *Briggflatts* especially, speak in what is believable as a direct, laconic personal voice, something nearly absent in his master Pound. Bunting's control of tone is exquisite through many emotional ranges, in a sparse body of work written over forty years where every single sound is carefully judged. The image of a language in his work is carried through heroic figures of kings and writers: the ideal language is masculine, cautious, abrupt, elegiac, as intricate and quirky as a Celtic illuminated manuscript, full of nouns as things and names.

Briefly near the end I show examples of how Bunting's ideal language can stand against the debasements of politics and journalism. This affords a slender social mooring. If I were writing this chapter now, I would not have such a Quaker and quietist final paragraph. The present chapter is exceeded by the book that surrounds it: a future Bakhtinian criticism, as started in my more recent chapters 1 and 5, would move in the direction of a fully developmental and social account, based on struggle between inner and outer speech.

After *dialogism* itself, Bakhtin's theory of *inner speech* deserves as much productive attention as *carnival* and *chronotope*. That Bakhtin should have conceived the idea of inner speech at the same time as Lev Vygotsky, independently but in parallel and in Russia, reinforces one's sense of a continuing collaborative project. A. N. Sokolov's monograph, *Inner Speech and Thought*[28] admirably tracks the Vygotsky side, following investigations of inner speech carried out in the Soviet Union since Vygotsky's book of 1934, and up to the 1970s. Sokolov's opening survey of philosophies of language serves to point up ways human speech and thought work in contrast; he argues that wordless thinking, which does exist, should more appropriately be called "verbal-pictorial" to show that words or their fragments are present (27). In his middle chapters Sokolov has much to say, often quoting and framing the remarks of Vygotsky, that might be productive in literary discussions: about images in creative thinking, about how inner speech is "the living process of the birth of thought in the word" (quoted in Vygotsky, 46), about how inner speech is compressed and fragmentary in comparison to external speech— sometimes just a predicate, about how "it is impossible to have two internal speeches going on simultaneously" (quoted Blonskii 53), and about experiments in speech interference that block concealed articulation and thus prove its presence (chapter 5). Generalizing in the final paragraph of this book, Sokolov makes a very large claim before he calls for further physiological research: "The material presented permits us to regard inner speech and the concealed articulation associated with it, as the principal mechanism of thought, with the aid of which there takes place goal-directed selection, generalization, and storage of sensory information. . . . Hence the enormous significance of inner speech not only in verbal-conceptual but also in concrete thinking, as well as in the formation and functioning of all voluntary acts of man. If this is true, then it is logical to assert that inner speech is a very important factor in human consciousness, verbal in its genesis, structure, and functioning" (263–64). Psychologists outside Russia most certainly know Vygotsky and work in his tradition, but Western students of physiology or of Freud do not to the same great extent concern themselves with speaking, or with the clash of inner and outer speech.

Within the literary field, my notes to this chapter tell the story of what has been done; perhaps my own most useful discovery in the text of the chapter is a small extension of the Russian ideas, as they might moor poetry to the social—on writing as revised inner speech, on "*editing* as a way in which inner speech is made social." Basil Bunting, we know, was a ferocious editor of his own thoughts and poems; he was hard on his inner life and speech as only a modernist could be hard, in the editing out of the merely personal or political. In this, he is more like the rhyme-and-meter track, civic poet Robert Pinsky as I describe Pinsky in the clash of discourses at the end of chapter 5, below: many artful exclusions of things thrusting at the text.

The other side of the clash in chapter 5 is also of interest here, because Charles Bernstein's poetry may seem to range itself against both Bunting and Pinsky in this matter of editing. Without worksheets, we will not know what changes any of these writers have made. However, in the presence of the poems themselves we may see Bernstein's concept of invention as a miming of inner speech within the poem—in the form of the very condensed and fragmentary speech the Russian psychologists postulated: more attention to the texture of inner speech, or the imagined texture, in sensory jumble, fragmentary thoughts, sentence particles, nonsense and non-euphonious sounds, a range of diction from the most colloquial Anglo-Saxon to the most pompous Latinate words. Bernstein's work appears less censored, and the politics of seeming not edited may be to use inner speech in its compression and seeming chaos as a challenge to arbitrary, official languages. For Bernstein, in his theoretical works and in writing related comment in his poems themselves, this denial of the appearance of editing is an exploration of the sources of language as language: he takes inner speech as thinking and ideology. For Bernstein, this is more artificial than the rhyme-and-meter civic language of a Pinsky or the sound loving editing of a Bunting, which gain accessibility by known public means. Innovation in politics and poetry requires that Bernstein go to the roots of sounds and meanings where they are still malleable, at play, not yet owned by a person. As I will argue in Chapter 5 and its notes, this is a viable and increasingly influential position in contemporary poetics; but it is a position Bakhtin cannot recognize, since Bakhtin, while he sanctions the slippage between thought and idea that makes for inner speech, cannot permit any slippage between utterance and person.

4

Rhythmic Cognition in the Reader: Bakhtin, Tsvetaeva, and the Social Moorings of Rhythm

In THIS BOOK, I ARGUE THAT BAKHTIN'S FAMOUS PROMOTION OF THE DIA-logic novel at the expense of monologic poetry can be explained and, if we are generous, forgiven. That this effacement of poetry is not a fundamental error is proved by the many excellent studies that use the terms of Bakhtin's system, with rather than against Bakhtin, to interpret speech acts in poetry. The fundamental error is else-where: what he and his circle and those working with his system have got wrong is the meaning and role of *poetic rhythm*, which is what makes poetry poetry. The philosopher of great time has misunder-stood the little time of human acts of attention.

A negative report designed to change the agenda should give the argument in its strongest form. However, to be fair to Bakhtin and critics who use his terms, I should say that usually I find their deal-ings with poetry admirable; I propose not critique but completion. Gary Saul Morson and Caryl Emerson, in their magisterial but po-lemical *Creation of a Prosaics*, are right to insist that while Bakhtin is "not immune to [an] imperializing move on behalf of the novel," in the light of prosaics poetics may seem "inadequate even for its own object, poetry," and once we "examine prose in its own terms, we will come to see all verbal art, poetry included, in a different way."[1] (At the end of this essay, I shall argue that if this is true, it is strictly reversible: prosaics recruits and corrects itself with ideas of rhythmic cognition invented in poetics.) Bakhtin, as Morson and Emerson admit, "never did fully work out" the implications of his approach for lyric poetry, and I agree, except that in my view given his premises he never could work that out, and we inherit the task. It can be worked out only with premises generated after Bakhtin's

97

death, by theorists of rhythm like Henri Meschonnic and Richard D. Cureton. The aim is to break through to a rhythmics, and *thence* to a dialogics of lyric poetry.

Bakhtin's own dealings with poetry and poetics are more extensive than we would think from an encounter with his essay, "Discourse in the Novel" (1934–35), and even in that essay I see gestures toward the end that partly modify the lyric-as-monologue claim of the opening; and that essay has an amazing number of passing references to poems. V. N. Voloshinov's poetry-friendly study of sociological poetics, "Discourse in Life and Discourse in Poetry" (1926), and Pavel Medvedev's *Formal Method in Literary Scholarship* (1928), were written while the enemy was still the detachable device rather than monologism. There, members of Bakhtin's Circle speak of the interrelation of style and social meanings; they are wise about intonation, about excessive theoreticism in stylistics and linguistics, about the mistake of an exclusive focus on poetic devices, about the co-participant role of the listener-reader. Bakhtin himself tends to admire epic and narrative poems, where style and sound are de-emphasized, but he does give two long, intelligent, early-twenties readings of the same personal lyric by Pushkin, "Parting" (*"Dlia beregov otchizny dal'- noi . . ."*): eleven pages at the end of *Towards a Philosophy of the Act*, and twenty pages in the supplementary section of "Author and Hero in Aesthetic Activity."[2] (I will return to apply his categories from these Pushkin readings in my own description of Marina Tsvetaeva's "Wires" [*Provoda*], a comparable poem on the theme of parting.)

My search for recent English-language studies of poetry that use Bakhtin's terminology and ideas has yielded over a hundred articles and several books, and these I would divide into utterance-intonation studies such as Don Bialostosky's book on Wordsworth, and heteroglossia studies with a political edge such as Robert Crawford's book on late twentieth-century world poetries in English.[3] Some of the articles cross this line and take up both local speech acts and also the clashes of official and unofficial languages. Typical titles are "Reading Pound With Bakhtin: Sculpting the Social Languages of *Hugh Selwyn Mauberly*," or "Marvell's Dialogics of History . . . ," or "John Clare's 'Childe Harold': A Polyphonic Reading." One of the most capacious of these articles is Lynn J. Shakinovsky's "Hidden Listeners: Dialogism in the Poetry of Emily Dickinson." Shakinovsky addresses the "powerful powerlessness" of many of Dickinson's speakers, their "efforts to gain monologic power, the illogicality of the texts, the split subject, and . . . the role of other suppressed voices in her poems." Through close readings of three poems, she shows how boundaries are blurred between reader and addressee inside the text, how the reader is "oddly implicated" even in the confusions—a poem's passive constructions, placement of dashes, or seemingly inept repetition of sounds. These are social aspects of the texts, and they display in language Dickinson's marginal existence as a woman and a poet. Briefly, with each of her examples, this critic refers to local effects of rhythm, but Shakinovsky is like all these articles and books, including my own, in largely avoiding the study of rhythmic phrasing. In over a thousand pages of Bakhtinian analysis, every one of us has preferred to ask who is speaking, rather than to ask about the multidimensional response-units of the reader, and has preferred ideologeme-reading to skills-reading, intonation to rhythm, versification to cognition, meter to the encompassing category of rhythm. Is *that* the contribution of prosaics to poetics? *Prosaics*, the increasingly popular term for Bakhtin's theory of the novel and of communication acts generally, is a neologism formed on (and against) the term *poetics*. To insist on the centrality of prosaics is to follow Bakhtin in relegating poetry and the theory of poetry; this allows us to map his thought on aesthetics, speech acts, and the novel. However, in our adhesion to his thought, our lack of dialogic distance, we are bound to repeat (or at least to miss seeing) his severe error, namely his inability to read poetry as an art of human expectation. Bakhtin flattens out and spatializes the theory of rhythm, and this, not his polemic praise of the novel, must be confronted first. Only then can we reconvert his prosaics back into a poetics of utterance, intonation, rhythmic phrasing, and history. In fact, Bakhtin is magnificent on the forms of meaning, but he is terribly conventional on the meanings of form; a full poetics will need to attend equally to, and coordinate, both these modes of understanding. (Actually, Bakhtin does that successfully in the audiotape readings of German poems, which were heard by delegates to the Moscow Conference in June 1995. Bakhtin reads poetry aloud with great understanding and power, but that performance is not pertinent here; it is his theory of reading that is currently at issue.)

Much (fortunately not all) of my argument rests on my example and what I can do with it. My analysis of Marina Tsvetaeva's "Wires" (*Provoda*) has less philosophical reach than Henri Meschonnic and less linguistic system than Richard Cureton; however, despite the limitations of one non-native surmise about rhythmic cognition in Russian, correcting Bakhtin's wrong turn will have *a priori* force, if it can be done with reference to a powerful countertheory. This is a case where having the better hypothesis is more important than providing a watertight, comprehensive analysis.

"Wires" is a diary poem in ten parts, written between mid March and early April 1923, and published in *After Russia* (*Posle Rossii*). The poems are intellectual love letters to Boris Pasternak, who was leaving Germany to return to the Russia that was forbidden to her. Lily Feiler's 1994 biography describes Tsvetaeva's frantic agitation during the early twenties, when the exiled poet conducted several epistolary romances, projecting to distant, largely imaginary addressees the image of herself as erotic heroine; Catherine Ciepiela takes this perception down into the weave of metaphors of necessary absence in the poems: "Tsvetaeva requires the absence of the beloved insofar as it involves the mediation of language."[4] Tsvetaeva was wounding herself into creativity: the writing of her early exile is *cri de coeur* poetry, as pure an instance as one might find of what Bakhtin considers self-regarding lyric, largely sealed off from the community by the self-isolation of the speech act and by the need to follow and derange a prescribed rhythmic pattern. If we could find elements of dialogism here, in such an extreme case, the discovery would help us to give equal privilege to poetry and prose.

I propose to make two attempts at a reading of the opening poem in "Wires." In my first pass through Tsvetaeva's poem, I will try to account for it by the pertinent, indeed profound, but also limited analytical categories Bakhtin uses to read Pushkin's "Parting," a poem of three eight-line stanzas. I believe these two congruent 1920s readings of the same poem are Bakhtin's only extensive readings of lyric. In my second attempt at reading Tsvetaeva, I will introduce a synthesis of terms and procedures more logically adequate from Yuri Tynianov, Henri Meschonnic, and the American proponent of rhythmic phrasing, Cureton. I will show that the more logically adequate terms and procedures are also more practical because they help us to account for more of Tsvetaeva's poem, and to read it as poetry and not, or as well as, something else.

In both of these fragmentary studies, Bakhtin analyzes Pushkin's "Parting" as an example, to enforce points made in the body of his argument. His readings are presented not as afterthoughts but as confirmatory shifts down from exposition to unusual (for him) depth of detail. In both studies he quotes the whole poem once in full, an admirable practice, and then quotes segments as he explains smaller units. In both studies he is as usual writing ethical and aesthetic theory in order to combat theoreticism. In both, he follows his habit of checking the philosophical or literary act against speech-acts in the world. The term *architectonic* appears prominently in both readings, as Bakhtin's way of relating the two unique places of the speaker and his departed, now dead, Italian lover Riznich. "The architectonic is *something-given* as well as *something-to-be-accomplished*, for it is the architectonic of an event," (*TPA* 75). Here the *event* is physical distance as a foreshadowing of metaphysical separation. *Contraposition* shows the *outsidedness* of lovers *vis à vis* one another, valuable because the only way we are defined is by others outside us in concrete moments of perception. *Outsidedness* makes self-definition possible, as Pushkin shows in the authorial gesture that unifies remembered times and the *now,* and unifies the present-day grieving speaker-hero and the time after his own death when he will redeem Riznich's promise of a kiss: "*No zhdu ego; on za toboi.*" In *Towards a Philosophy of the Act,* whose analysis I have just given, Bakhtin says that the speaker and his lover are subordinated to Pushkin's authorial context, an author-preference he pushes harder in the "Author and Hero" essay.

In "Author and Hero" he refers to "Parting" as "this basically understandable poem," I suppose because he can find in it an opposition, which he pursues at length, between *intonation* and *formal intonation* in the lyric: "The intonation of almost every word in the poem must be performed in three directions: the real-life intonation of the heroine and of the hero, and the formal intonation of the author/reader," who integrates the different places, times, and points of view, from a standpoint external to them (*AH* 212–13). In fact, the later "Author and Hero" takes a less cautious view of these matters; while *Towards a Philosophy of the Act* ends its analysis and whole argument with the view that the I-Other contraposition produces "an equivocation, a contradiction between form and content," "Author and Hero" openly prefers real life to formal intention, and sets *intonation* against and above *rhythm.*

At one point earlier in "Author and Hero," Bakhtin explicitly formulates the relationship of rhythm and intonation, those two processes that cannot be notated and that, as he says, must be "surmised." Bakhtin says:

> The sound-image of a word is not only the bearer of rhythm, but is also
> thoroughly permeated by intonation, and in the actual reading of a work
> conflicts may arise between intonation and rhythm. . . . Rhythm repre-
> sents, almost exclusively, a purely formal reaction of the author to the
> event as a *whole*, whereas intonation is . . . the intonational reaction of
> the *hero* to an object *within* the whole and . . . it is internally more differ-
> entiated and diversified." (*AH* 215–216).

Here, in order to show "the internal rhythm of the event," Bakhtin actually uses a term from old-fashioned technical metrics: "The
parting is the *arsis*, the promised meeting is the *thesis*; death is the
arsis, yet there will be a meeting, nevertheless—the *thesis*" (*AH* 215).
This is unhelpful; I do not object to Bakhtin's account of the poem's
multiple times and persons, but to the way he takes rhythm as meter
and meter as a structural principle of alternation, extendable to
huge nonlinguistic structures in the text. Here, on this page, Bakhtin needs to see rhythm as a "purely formal reaction of the author,"
separable from thought and language and their reception by a
reader. This resonates with his disparagement of rhythm within the
body of the "Author and Hero" essay, where he says the author as
creator is free and active but rhythm is unfree: "My relation to myself is incapable of being rhythmical. . . . In rhythm, as under narco-
sis, I am not conscious of myself" (*AH* 120). From here, it is but a
short step to the outright denunciation of rhythm in "Discourse in
the Novel," a decade later:

> *Rhythm by creating an unmediated involvement between every aspect of the accen-*
> *tual system of the whole* . . . destroys in embryo those social worlds of speech
> and of persons that are potentially embedded in the word. . . . Rhythm
> serves to strengthen and concentrate even further the unity and her-
> metic quality of the surface of poetic style, and of the unitary language
> that this style posits.[5]

Everything that a refutation has to confront is in this passage: the
emphasis on the author and the device, not on the reader's cognition; the allegation that rhythm is solely individual and monologic,
not social; and the sense that rhythm is a surface effect, and thus
detachable. Usually Bakhtin is more shaded and nuanced than that,
yet the passage does show his basic position.
    Bakhtin might have analyzed Tsvetaeva, because "Wires" dates
1923, almost exactly the moment of the two essays with pages on

Pushkin; of course, geopolitics and literary politics were against it.
But if he had done it, he would have described first the separation
of speaker from her addressee and the slender link between them,
that is the telegraph wire. Here is the first of ten diary-dated poems
in "Wires":

1

In a row of singing pillars,
Supporting the Empyrean,
I send to you my share
Of the dale dust.
     Along the alley
Of sighs—with a wire to a pole—
A telegraphic: I lo—o—ve . . .

I plead . . . (a printed blank
Won't fit it! It is simpler with wires!)
These are pillars, on them Atlas
Lowered a race track
Of Olympian gods . . .
     Along the pillars
A telegraphic fa—are—well . . .

Do you hear? This is the last breakdown
Of a torn off throat: fa—are—well . . .
These are riggings above a sea of fields,
The quiet Atlantic path:

Higher, higher—and we mer—ged
In Ariadne's: re—turn,

Turn around! . . . The melancholy
Of charity hospitals: I won't get out!
In the farewells of steel wires
Are the voices of Hades

Moving away . . . Conjuring
The distance: pi—ty . . .

Pity me! (In this chorus you will notice
It?) In the death rattle

Of obstinate passions is
The breath of Eurydice:

Through mounds and ditches
Eurydice's: a—a—las,

Don't lea—

March 17

1

Вереницею певчих свай,
Подпирающих Эмпиреи,
Посылаю тебе свой пай
Праха дольнего.
    По аллее
Вздохов--проволокой к столбу--
Телеграфное: лю--ю--блю…

Умоляю… (печатный бланк
Не вместит! Проводами проще!)
Это--сваи, на них Атлант
Опустил скаковую площадь
Небожителей…
    Вдоль свай
Телеграфное: про--о--щай…

Слышишь? Это последний срыв
Глотки сорванной: про--о--стите…
Это--снасти над морем нив,
Атлантический путь тихий:

Выше, выше,--и сли--лись
В Ариаднино: ве--ер--нись,

Обернись!.. Даровых больниц
Заунывное: не выйду!
Это--проводами стальных
Проводов--голоса Аида

Удаляющиеся... Даль
Заклинающее: жа--аль...

Пожалейте! (В сем хоре--сей
Различаешь?) В предсмертном крике
Упирающихся страстей--
Дуновение Эвридики:

Через насыпи--и--рвы
Эвридикино: у--у--вы,

Не у--
17 марта 1923

Bakhtin would have shown that the speaker is here in exile, and that she implores her addressee not to return to Russia; this is a very different spatial-national issue from what occurs in the Pushkin poem. Exile is a non-home for Tsvetaeva's hero, and she had hoped to make it into an international art-home, with Pasternak nearby as co-equal creator/lover/listener/critic: to amplify this, Bakhtin would have quoted Tsvetaeva's early-twenties prose letter to Pasternak, calling him "brother in the fifth season and the fourth dimension " (quoted in Feiler, 141). He would have made something of the metaphor in the title: "Wires" of the telegraph are fragile lines of contact, needing brevity and prohibiting touch. Studying the poem's pattern of intonation, Bakhtin might have shown how Russia, left behind by the speaker but now Pasternak's object of desire, determines every feeling in the poem. Tsvetaeva's best single book, which includes "Wires," is entitled aggressively and despairingly *After Russia*, and Bakhtin could well define just those tones of voice, registering the violent self preoccupation of the speaker and the oddly naked dialogism of her private verse-letter printed in a public book. Since he explicitly speaks in praise of series-poems in the Pushkin passage in "Author and Hero," Bakhtin would have appreciated the way a larger narrative is started with this first letter-poem.

All to the good! Bakhtin would have seen a lot, though I suspect he would be slightly shocked at the degree of lyric monologic intensity here.

Remember now Bakhtin's typical and quietly dramatic statement in chapter 5, section 4 of his book on *The Formal Method*: "Only the utterance can be beautiful, just as only the utterance can be true or false, bold or timid" (84). In his wish to rehabilitate the primary speech genres, he can do so only at the expense of secondary authorship. For him, monologism is an exaggeration of secondary, properly literary authorship, and lyric poetry, which is in the first person and employs metrical rhythm, is an exaggeration of monologism. Rhythm in this scheme is an abstraction from real experience and a restriction of freedom.

But what if we turn Bakhtin on his head, and with him virtually the entire tradition of work on Russian and English prosody? What if we focus not on versification—the text—but on verse rhythm—the reader? The alternative twentieth-century tradition I am sketching here begins with Tynianov's book *The Problem of Verse Language*, (1924) with his statement that once admitted into verse, *every* phonetic element becomes "rhythmicized," and his demonstration that an artistic device is a relationship of "complex interaction, not conjunction": in effect, a *struggle* between rhythm and syntax, not their cooperation.[7] Focused on the device, Tynianov did not develop his intuition concerning how the reader attends to larger discursive form. The next major step in my story is Émile Benveniste's 1951 essay "The Notion of Rhythm in its Linguistic Expression" (1951). I read Benveniste through his disciple Meschonnic, who says that after Benveniste "rhythm can no longer be a subcategory of form. It is an organization (disposition, configuration) of an *ensemble* . . . If rhythm is an organization of sense in a discourse, it is no longer a distinct, juxtaposed level."[8] Meschonnic develops Tynianov and Benveniste in *Critique du rhythme*, where he argues that "If sense is an activity of the subject, if rhythm is an organization of sense in discourse, rhythm is necessarily an organization or configuration of the subject in his or her discourse" (70–71). Meschonnic does not perform many sample analyses in over seven hundred pages; his task is not to develop a notation or to analyze poems, but to criticize a tradition of linguistic poetics and to propose a new heading. His first aim is to use the subject-tied nature of rhythm to refute Roman Jakobson's linguistics of the sign; but another explicit aim (to which he devotes twenty pages) is to break down Bakhtin's dualism of prose and poetry. Rhythm is an organization of large and small unities, inseparable from syntax, sense, and value in the poem; whereas "metrics," says Meschonnic, "is the rhythm-theory of imbeciles"

(143). Individual, collective, new in each poem, rhythm is the orality of a discourse; rhythm is the way the body gets into language and the way the spoken gets into the written. Thus it is profoundly political.

This story of an alternative tradition ends with Richard Cureton's *Rhythmic Phrasing in English Verse*, a book that takes its origins in cognitive psychology and music theory.[9] For Cureton, rhythmic shape creates our experience of time in the poem: "The simultaneous arrays of projected beats, culminating groups and completing regions that constitute rhythmic structure define shapes of cognitive and physiological energy, shapes that, taken collectively and in concert, are some of the most precise analogues of our emotional energies" (Cureton 426). As with Meschonnic, rhythm here is multidimensional, top-down, and an effect of discourse. But Cureton goes far beyond Meschonnic to validate intuitions about meter ("our rhythmic response to regular pulsations in a perceptual medium"), grouping ("our rhythmic response to points of structural culmination within delimited structural spans"), and prolongation ("our rhythmic response . . . to anticipated points of structural resolution/completion") (Cureton 124–25). For him, phrasal phenomena such as caesura and enjambment are more universal and expressively powerful than metrical forms.

Cureton takes his first 118 pages to describe the severe limitations of current approaches and to refute the myths of traditional prosody, then another hundred fifty-eight to define rhythmic competence and his key variables of meter, grouping, and prolongation, and to specify what he calls grouping well-formedness rules, always demoting meter as the least powerful variable in favor of mind-in-time, as we recognize patterns of anticipation, arrival, and recursive understanding of the whole poem. In his longest chapter, "Analysis," he then exhaustively analyzes examples of free verse, sprung rhythm, and pentameter; and he concludes with a short chapter of only eighteen pages on implications for pedagogy and criticism. I have described the book's contents to show that Cureton performs all the necessary logics of critique, affinity-finding, definition, notation-proposing, and context-building to deliver a complete theory. The "Analysis" chapter is crucial because there Cureton shows how a single method can describe three poems extremely different in structure. For example, his analysis of Gerard Manley Hopkins's "Windhover" sonnet shows the poem syllable by syllable in a horizontal/vertical tree diagram; Cureton then reads the poem through eleven levels of phrasing from the whole poem down to the syllable; then he shows centroidal groupings by deleting down from the highest levels; finally, he analyzes line by metrical line to rebuild the reader's apprehension of the whole. Cureton's back-and-forth is unwieldy but impressively complete in its reimagining of the reader's thought processes. To demonstrate Cureton's method here would require that the protocols be performed for all ten poems of Tsvetaeva's "Wires" series, showing the role of each poem within the series—plainly impossible because it would require hundreds of pages for grouping reductions and line by line analyses. Instead, I offer one person's reading of Tsvetaeva justified by Meschonnic's arguments and influenced by Cureton's definitions and method; an attempt to recapture, and turn into a narrative account, the experience of grouping, meter, and prolongation in the first poem of "Wires," taking that poem as representative and offering perceptions on how it opens, and thus links itself to the rest of the series.

Let us return then to "Wires." If we consider rhythmic intent, which subsumes intonation, these are not just love letters to Pasternak, these are white-hot telegrams, abrupt, violent, jammed in phrasing for economy and frequently broken in transmission. Tsvetaeva's brevity is motivated by the idea of telegraphic concision. She can hardly utter a syllable, word, or phrase without throttling it, or imagining that telegraph technology has re-segmented her language, or diminished it within a "chorus" ("voices" [line 22]; "chorus" [line 25]) of other speakers who are crowding onto the same lines. "Wires 1," unlike the other nine in the series, ends with a broken stanza, broken line, broken word: "Don't lea—," must be completed by the reader as "Don't leave." The silent deleted syllables rouse a strong completion syndrome in the reader, leading to the other nine telegrams-letters-cries-dated diary entries-death rattles, those Tsvetaevan speech genres of extremity, all of which do more than imply or apostrophize—they *grasp* and *bully* the addressee, who is Pasternak in the first instance but also, always, the reader amazed at the controlled violence of the utterance. This one moment at the end of the first poem, a jagged, premature closure that forces the reader's collaboration and thus intensifies and does not conclude the reader's mental energy, may lead us to the first of Cureton's categories of rhythmic hearing, what he calls grouping. This category preeminently requires harvesting the poem recursively, both ways from the center or backwards from the ending.

Grouping. We are discussing the rapport between a protagonist and her reader, and if we now move to reader-oriented strategies, the flow of conscious experience can be divided into large strong-weak oppositions across the poem as a whole. The reader registers through shifts of intonation and metaphor that Tsvetaeva begins with images of telegraph lines and of herself as hero, but she ends on a bald declaratory statement, having stripped off self-display. Other overarching oppositions are part of grouping at the higher levels of intonation or metaphor: the height of telegraph wires against the sky versus the lowness of valley-dust (first two stanzas); "singing pillars" of line 1 versus Hades of line 22 and the underworld "mounds and ditches" of Euridice at end; high clarity of a "torn off throat" in the third (six-line) stanza versus subsumption in the chorus of the fifth; Euridice (Tsvetaeva) versus Orpheus (Pasternak); the sending and questioning verbs of the first three stanzas versus the begging verbs of the fifth and sixth ("Pity me!"; "Don't lea—"); and within each stanza, the quatrain's narrative or vaunt versus the attached couplet's broken words and raw expression of need. More at the end than at the high detached opening, the speaker's language is crumbling and reverting to matter, under pressure of feeling. When the speaker flings down that broken word-line stanza at the end (line 31 is a nascent, incomplete stanza), she leaves a garbled, incomplete message, and intonation units, already tiny in this poem, get even smaller toward the poem's final part-line.

Cureton finds centroidal patterns in the reader's temporal-semantic registration of the poem: my noticing of the relation of four-line to two-line segments within each stanza, the difference in rhetoric and intent, is just what he would claim is typical of a poet like Tsvetaeva, who divides even her smaller building blocks by further divisions. However, I see in Tsvetaeva another, far more unusual pattern, possibly unique to this poem and very much part of the rhetoric of its use of shortening intonation units in the line. One notes that hardly a single sentence is coincident with a line; it is sometimes even doubtful whether there *is* a sentence, whether there *is* a line. This instability is exaggerated by other devices: of thirty-one lines, twenty are broken by typographical step-down, or by dashes, colons, or suspension dots. There are mid-line and near-end-of-line breaks in lines already miniature, breaks within breaks and turns within turns. In fact, starting at the end of the first stanza, the poem tends to break in half *vertically, down the middle of each line.* The reader lur-

ches from half-line to half-line, from line to line, word to word, syllable to syllable. This would be a strenuous enough rhetoric in
cognition, but we must also register at the same time what is woven
in semantically in changes of speech act, allusions to literary and
mythical figures, and leaps from the grotesque to the sublime from
one line to another (for example, from charity hospitals to Hades).
Tsvetaevan poetic grouping (as intonation, syntactic focus and the-
matic ornament) connives at maximum instability; Tsvetaevan time
comes in a flurry of tiny units, which frequently change direction
and manner of linkage before and behind.

Meter. When our concern is for rhythmic phrasing (for the archi-
tecture of the brain, and for the way humans pay attention to time
within the verbal arts) meter loses its preeminence in versification;
meter becomes one among several patterns of expectation to which
we attend simultaneously. Rhythm cannot, although this is what
Bakhtin seems to have argued, be reduced to meter. Rather, meter
actualizes and reinforces rhythm. The binary and ternary meters in
Tsvetaeva's short lines are combined in harsh and unexpected ways
as part of the baffling of expectation produced. The intonation
units are subdivided, and syntax is jammed or inverted in order to
get rhymes on the same number syllable in the line. Russian's avoidance of the forms of the verb "to be," and the consequent replacement with "*eto*" (this/it/these/they [is/are]) in the middle line of
the three middle stanzas in the poem, gives a rare beginning-of-line
stress and sets up an unusual line that strives to right itself by the
end of its short run. None of the "*eto*" lines ends with one of the
eight line-final pauses in the middles of words (for instance, line 6,
"*liu—iu—bliu;*" "I lo—o—ve"). These words are highly unusual in
producing hyperprosodic stresses: the dividing dashes call for addi-
tional stress, but when this happens, Simon Karlinsky well says, Tsvetaeva "violate[s] the very basis of Russian prosody by requiring
more than one stress per word."[10] If this happened once it would be
an event with no implication for rhythmic phrasing; but it happens
eight times at similar end-line positions, creating a stutter-like refrain, a metrical effect that is part of the rhythmic punctuation of
the poem, a sound effect that underscores the public nature of the
telegram medium, its slippages away from the ideal of lyric intensity.
When the poem is a telegram, the dash can be a metrical device and
words can revert to their non sense constituents. Thus across the
grid of a fairly stable metrical structure and rhyme scheme (lines

like wires) Tsvetaeva has written with punctuational excess, lexical instability,[11] and deliberate syntactic uncertainty. From the smallest particles of language, morphemes, through the volatile rank of the relation of line and sentence, up to the overall plot of failure to say farewell, this is "The last breakdown / Of a torn off throat" (lines 13–14); this is a rhythm of rude wrenching.

Prolongation. While grouping and meter tend to be recursive, summative, overarching, prolongation of the reader's attentional energies points forward: "It divides the text into a hierarchy of prolongational *regions,* each of which is defined by a point of structural *arrival/departure"* (Cureton 146). Hardly any of Tsvetaeva's lines and stanzas is stopped by syntax or full period punctuation, so the poem's movement would seem headlong—except for the mid-line checks mentioned above; we get lurches from mid-line to mid-line, with quick turns at line-ends. Or we get words or part-words isolated as the line's last unstable syllable (lines 6, 12, 17, 18, 23, 24, 25, 29, 30, 31), an effect of toppling over the ends of lines; but this particular prolongation is often stymied by an imperative the next line down: an "arrival" at a new badgering verb (in one case playing on the Russian: *zh—al' / Pozhal*eite!). The poem exaggerates transition by its stanza- and line-ends, and blocks transition by its line-starts and mid-line breaks, yielding stop-start stutter effects. Prolongational and metrical devices move in parallel with shortened intonational groupings, to saturate the reader's attentional energies. By these means, emblems of the force of her desire, the speaker attempts to eliminate the distance between herself and Pasternak, herself and the reader.

Tsvetaeva is Euridice telling Orpheus not to go, but she is a poet also—and first. The ten sections of "Wires" persistently raise oppositions between Euridice versus Orpheus, lips and arms versus writing, talking versus telegraphing. These are resolved, along with the paradox of distance between Tsvetaeva's exile-Hell and Pasternak's Russia, in the tenth poem's weird, daring assertion of a child born of Pasternak and the author, an illusionary creation that will rival natural birth. This is Tsvetaeva's final vaunt and hyperbole, sent out on telegraph wires to conquer them.

To come this far with the rhythms of "Wires" is, I submit, to have done much to complete what was partial in Bakhtin's response to verse. To push this logic just one step further, however, we can say that Bakhtin has a tendency to state that poetry was the prestige form of an earlier era, and that the novel is the form of modernity. This is a history of genres that contributes to the effacement of poetry by the novel. But what if we replay the logic of my argument in reverse? If Bakhtin (and most of his Circle, his followers, his students) can be so wrong about the reader's developing attention in the time of the poem, how can study of the novel claim to *come after*? Narratology has not theorized its own reading practice at the skills level, and lacks a terminology of grouping and prolongation with which to describe the movement of feeling in the novel. Perhaps one sour revenge of poetry and rhythmic phrasing will be to teach students of narrative how to read, and to teach philosophers how to be critics and to know what we actually *do* when we read.

AFTERWORD 2002

This chapter was written during an eight hour train journey from St. Petersburg to Moscow, on the way to the 1995 conference where I presented it in short bursts that were translated directly into Russian by the magnificent Igor Shakhinovsky. Its germ was in a sentence in a letter to me by Richard D. Cureton, protesting that Bakhtin and his American follower Don H. Bialostosky have a conventional, and entirely starved, idea of rhythm. This still seems to me correct on the grounds of poetic technique, where I argued the case here; but I now think there is more to be said on the matter, to develop a wider range of Bakhtin's statements about rhythm, and to adjust this study to my theme of the social moorings of poetry.

Already in this afterword I have invoked the manifolds of space (journey) and time (re-thinking after a gap). Rhythm in the usual dictionary definitions is in the first instance a temporal pattern in all art forms, and by extension it is also spatial for all the senses except smell. Rhythm in the arts is already a question of profound complexity, subject to premature syntheses like Bakhtin's mistake of identifying poetic rhythm with poetic meter, or like James H. Bunn's ingenious and example-filled, but fatally flawed recent book, *Wave Forms*.[12] However, to reach beyond the boundaries of this chapter, rhythm is also a theological and political study, as I hope to suggest by further reference to Bakhtin and to Henri Meschonnic. With this range of meanings, rhythm is a classic instance of an essentially contested concept, which tempts some inquirers to common sense, reductive answers to naïve questions, and may lead others to find at least one productive question. I trust this polemical chapter's positive claims are not naïve, but certainly they are more partial than they need to be if I add a further request, for a beginning sketch of the social moorings of rhythm.

This chapter remains lucky in its choice of example. Marina Tsvetaeva, in a different poem from the one analyzed here, writes: "The poet takes up her speech from afar."[13] She too, like Bakhtin, invokes space, distance, perspective; this speech travels far enough to represent other social selves, other rhetorics.[14] She too, Bakhtin's contemporary, is born in one era and after 1917 lives into another, and thus knows herself to be vividly historical. On the showing of these writers born in the 1890s, it is possible to venture that the post-revolutionary speaking subject is not a static thing, but rather a place of competing discourses. The moment is a volatile one in which the middle-class self, with all its cults of interiority, has to remake itself or be remade in a new collectivist era. Tsvetaeva and Bakhtin held to pre-revolutionary personal and cultural values, but Soviet history cut scars into their themes and made them both exiles. A commentary on the whole period is Tsvetaeva's departure from the Soviet Union in the early twenties, after which her next collection's title was *After Russia*; then was the abandonment of her work by official Soviet culture until the late 1980s: mocked by Mayakovsky, not taught in faculties of Soviet literature, not published, but widely read, passionately admired. "Allegorical" is Henri Meschonnic's term for her, in his several long presentations of her work as a leading twentieth century example of the politics of rhythm.[15] Michael Makin argues that Tsvetaeva's whole production is a rewriting of inherited texts; but while he has massive evidence on the poetics of "source-saturated" (8) appropriation, he skirts Meschonnic's and my question: How does the historical speaking subject assert herself through rhythm, in its several senses and at all levels?[16]

I would like to get to the historical and Meschonnic, by working forward through the theological and Bakhtin. Although Meschonnic uses eight blistering pages to refute Bakhtin on the monologism of poetry in his *Critique du rythme: anthropologie historique du language* (1982), it does seem to me that his politics of rhythm in this book and in *Politique du rythme: politique du sujet* (1995) are the completion of an arc of thought begun in Bakhtin. My chapter 4, by grouping all Bakhtin's most clearly incorrect accounts of poetic rhythm from three separate pieces written between 1920 and 1934, loses a good deal of specific surrounding argumentation and loses a certain historical curve. Briefly to replace what I have omitted, I would bring in summary statements from Graham Pechey, the most valuable recent commentator on Bakhtin on rhythm. In two essays of stunning synthesis, Pechey explains the theological cast of the idea of rhythm, and the replacement of *rhythm* by *dialogue* in Bakhtin's work after the 1920s, once the limitations of the idea have become clear. This story of Bakhtin's self-correction is a story of social mooring of rhythm, which extends and supplements my narrow concerns in the chapter.

In "Philosophy and Theology in 'Aesthetic Activity'" (1998, 2001), Pechey focuses on the "Author and Hero in Aesthetic Activity" essay written by Bakhtin sometime between 1920 and 1923.[17] He finds a point in Bakhtin's long essay where the young Bakhtin, he says, invites us onto a ladder to "epiphanic states" and "sublime moments of individual and universal ending" (55): the ladder is "aesthetic activity [as] an everyday ritual" (55), upwards to death or apocalypse, downwards to "ethical-aesthetic activity at work in *this* world" (55). Pechey writes: "The word that Bakhtin uses for this aesthetic consummation of an inner life in time is *rhythm*. Only in the rhythm of aesthetic activity is any lived experience in the other freed from the future of meaning. . . . Rhythm installs meaning immanently within the lived experience. . . . Sin in Bakhtin's ethical-aesthetic sense is the absurd presumption that I can, as it were, 'rhythmicize' my own life. Faith is the rightfully insane belief against all odds that I do not coincide with myself" (55). That is, omitting much of Pechey's detail and subtlety, Bakhtin's mistake in thinking rhythm is something regular, formally recurrent, is here in a theological context pushed into a judgment that aesthetic pattern and closure are an analogy for sin, for denial of lived experience; aesthetic consummation is not grace. After several excellent pages on Bakhtin's vision of dance as the best of the rhythmic arts, "where art and the holy and the everyday meet" (Pechey's 58), Pechey in a passage on confession writes some sentences that lead us back to Tsvetaeva: "[Bakhtin] suggests very strongly the transhistorical power of confessional self-accounting when he claims that the characteristic forms of modern writing are merely confession diverted or perverted: irony and cynicism can be traced to confession that has a theomachic or anthropomachic cast, fighting against the judgment of God or man or both. Confession's worst perversion is invective, which utters in tones of malice all that the other might utter penitentially about herself, marking her as the one who *has no other"* (59–60). Tsvetaeva's "Wires" from a theological point of view is a form of ecstatic despair, that the love relation with Pasternak will be attenuated to humming wires: since she is about to have no other as a body or even an addressee, her lines and words must literally stretch to breaking. Those are the social moorings of this broken theological rhythm.

Graham Pechey's contribution to the 2001 Gdańsk conference is about literary seeing, as a latent but unexpressed term in Bakhtin's early thinking.[18] He writes: "To uncover the architectonics of literary seeing is . . . not to specialize 'literature' as a sub-set of the general category of the aesthetic, but rather to bring into view the aesthetic moment in *any* act of language" (MS p. 2). Pechey finds that literary seeing, architectonics, and rhythm disappear from Bakhtin's early writings at about the time of the late 1920s Dostoevsky book, when "he acknowledges in the novel a specific architectonics and not just a compositional variant of epic. . . . Quite simply, the Dostoevsky book marks the decisive undoing of this notably leaky opposition [between formal intonation and realistic rhythm, Baktin's own terms]. For what else is the polyphonic novel but a name for the limiting case of the free interchange . . . of exactly these counterposed attributes of rhythmic or intonational 'formality' and 'realism'? The interpenetration of rhythm and intonation, first implicitly ascribed to 'hybrid' genres like autobiography, is at length generalized to the novel as such under the sign of (what else?) *dialogism*. . . . It is tempting to say that with this move first an existential and then a sociological conception of the author replaces a quasi-theological one; but it is misleading. . . . Better, though, to say that these dimensions thrive only in the tension of each other's company" (MS pp. 7–8). So by another route Bakhtin came to surpass the earlier notion of rhythm that I criticized in my chapter. If Pechey is correct, the existential, theological, and sociological coexist in Bakhtin's thinking after 1930—so to drop any one of these perspectives might be legitimate, but not in the spirit of Bakhtin.

Given his training and prejudices, Bakhtin never worked out a fully social description of rhythm. However, he does share some premises with Henri Meschonnic, the linguist and philosopher who did. They both are opponents of Saussurian theoreticism and the tyranny of the structuralist idea of the sign; they both explore as a

116   BAKHTIN AND THE SOCIAL MOORINGS OF POETRY

research program the status of orality, as the spoken within the written. The inadequate sentences on Meschonnic in my chapter offer a drastic summary of a distinguished career devoted to these topics, and here in an afterword I cannot do justice to his thirteen hundred pages on the social moorings of rhythm in two huge books. Since I refer to Meschonnic in the chapter only in the context of critique of Bakhtin, and since his critique and reconceptualization of rhythm have been neglected outside France, I do wish to add something about his own positive achievement.[19]

It is fascinating that rhythm, so long misunderstood and marginalized, should become the focus of an argument that speaks for the primacy of discourse over language, of semantics over signs. In *Critique du rythme*, Henri Meschonnic writing twenty years ago thinks structuralism is even then past its productive moment; he everywhere wars with what he considers a false scientism that would reduce rhythm to meter or to the sign, reduce rhythm to a time that is "Kantian, homogeneous, linear, mathematizable" (21). Rhythm's recurrences are not like those of waves or heartbeats or metrical stresses, because the whole human subject is in motion, and rhythm is in the utterance and the discourse, part of the sense: "If sense is an activity of the human subject, if rhythm is an organization of sense in discourse, rhythm is necessarily an organization or configuration of the subject in his or her discourse" (71); "When rhythm is inseparably the syntax, the sense, and the value of a poem, it is its form-sense, its historicity. It transforms writing and literature. It imposes a new perception, and at a level not yet conceptualized by our culture" (357). The point is that only a rhythmics of discourse can renew rhythm; only a metrics of discourse can renew metrics. We need to bring into studies of poetry, in a responsible manner, syntax, the human subject, semantics, history, and politics: "A poetics and politics of individuation is at stake" (13).

Precisely because rhythm is a critique of sense, we require an adequate definition of rhythm. Meschonnic's second book directly on this topic, *Politique du rythme, politique du sujet* (1995), moves from a refutation of past theories to a defense and exposition of how rhythm can be a critique of the sign—the sign as the disgrace of theoreticism. We need, then, "to think a politics of rhythm outside the politics of the sign. And the poetizations of poetry, the joint essentializations of poetry and politics, even those that seem to rebel against the sign, will on the contrary only serve to assure the reign of the sign" (37). Here as in his separate book on *Le Langage Heidegger* (1990), Meschonnic is thinking of Heidegger as one who errs by essentializing, by a myth of ideal (in his case, German as Greek-loving) language. "The critique of rhythm does not *have* a politics, it *is* a politics" (41). "But poetry, perhaps, is the maximal historicization of the I, or a maximal subjectivization of language. The furthest reach of the ordinary. The exterior made intimate" (79). "The politics of rhythm emphatically does not mean a direct party-loyalty [*prise de parti*] politics, but rather the request for a constant mediation between—let it be said emblematically—poem, ethics, and politics" (155). Marina Tsvetaeva is a heroic example of "maximum possible subjectivity" (457) and freedom, for Meschonnic, where her discovery of her own rhythm is her discovery of, not herself, but her subjectivity: "this tension between prosody and rhythm, in Tsvetaeva . . . is not only not borrowed from metrics, but cancels out metrics by a rhythmics of excess. What's most characteristic of her poetry is rhythmic extremity, the coordinated play of accented monosyllables one right after another. Counter-accents . . . from a level beating-back upon the unaided sense of the words. Her sense is her rhythm" (462). Following Meschonnic's lead, I hope to have shown this in some detail, in my interpretation of the first poem in the "Wires" sequence. Meschonnic, even in books this long, does not offer an elaborated notation for reading rhythm or a pedagogical plan for tracking politics in typical turns of phrase, but he is original, and correct, to insist (75) that we should not orient ourselves in the politics of the poem—we should rather orient ourselves poetically within politics. Afterword as prospectus: What if we were to orient ourselves thus, starting there to read with Bakhtin, for discourse as rhythmic sense, dialogue, speaking subjects, clash of inner and outer speech, intonation, images of language?

5

Clash of Discourses in English Romanticism and the American 1990s

> The point of view from the outside, its character as surplus, and its boundaries. The point of view from the inside, upon itself. In which we cannot, on principle, counterpose the one against the other, we cannot merge. Exactly in this moment of non-coincidence, and not in a spirit of unification (indifferent to the internal and external points of view) events accomplish themselves. The continuing struggle, in the process of self-knowing, between the I and the other.
>
> —Bakhtin[1]

> The image of a discourse cannot be, at one and the same time, the image of a speaking human being.
>
> —Bakhtin[2]

CONTESTING DISCOURSES WITHIN THE PERIOD 1789–1815, AND WITHIN RECENT COMMENTARY ON THAT PERIOD

WHY IS IT USEFUL TO SEE THE PERIOD STYLE OF A WHOLE ERA (OF CRITI-cism, of poetry) divided into a clash of discourses? If we can show the main struggles with precision, we can also show the conceptual blends more successfully; we can characterize the era as an era—the pattern of the divisions, sometimes a dialogue and sometimes a conflict, specific to one time and no other time. Writers of one era, who contest with each other in clashes actual or implied, are divided over real issues, as they try to show forth a more complete version of the reality. Discourses also jostle, and contest for dominance within any historical moment, between and within single writers and groups of writers. How, then, define an era? How give a narrative of struggle for dominance—or a narrative of contemporaneous jostling? How validate *complete, version, reality,* and *narrative* as analytical terms?

In this final chapter, my perspective is wide because the vantage I have chosen is high. Although I will give some attention to four poems by four writers, in two pairs for comparison, my interest is mostly on the broad, image-of-a-language end, and not on the speaking-subject opening of the range that I set out in chapter 1. I am attempting to define the available English discourses within the post-French Revolution period, as these are in turn picked up and understood according to the available discourses of the Cold War and post-1989 period in Anglo-American criticism. The clash of discourses involves the biases of writers and critics within their own dense historical conditions of possibility, their own *combinatoires*. To ask a question Lucien Goldmann used to put to the absolute monarchy era of Pascal and Racine: for each of the times that interest us, what is the maximum possible consciousness? For us in the astounding era leading up to and beyond the historical break at 1989, how does writing develop its own pattern of bias and discovery, as we try to comb apart the discourses of the revolutionary era after 1789? What does our own era's condition of possibility help us to see and select, from first generation Romantic poetry, written two hundred years ago? Are we bound to be less exact—even less honest—the closer we come to the present, so that clash-of-discourses study is appropriate for a vertical plunge in time but not for a horizontal survey of what's going on now? Those would seem to be the right questions.[3]

William Hazlitt, that keen radical, said that Wordsworth's poetry caught on to the spirit of their age, a trend toward social justice that invigorated English politics by contagion of the French example after 1789, and even after the Terror and the king-killing and the increasing political distance between England and France in the period 1795–1802. Hazlitt said of Wordsworth that the poet's muse was a leveling one, populist, open to all. Shelley, Browning, and others in the nineteenth century disagreed, calling Wordsworth a lost leader, but it has taken until the last generation of criticism—in Marxism and New Historicism since about 1980—for Wordsworth to be impugned as a Burkean conservative who displaced into aesthetics, and into the idealism of nature-religion, his early revolutionary commitment. This is a well known story in the commentary on Romanticism, which I repeat here to remind the reader how difficult it is to make statements about maximum possible consciousness when: 1) we have not yet engaged in a massive rehearsal of the forces in conflict in the period after 1789, different in each nation, each class, each race, and in the lives of women; and when, 2) we have not engaged, either, the forces in conflict in our own period that open some approaches to the earlier period and close off others, and that prevent us even from seeing forces in conflict in our time when we are living them. Like First Generation Romantics and all others since, we have hope and even some knowledge upon which to base projections, but we cannot judge which groups and ideas will be historical victors. After reading critics such as Alan Liu, James Chandler, Marjorie Levinson, and Kenneth R. Johnston, I think we must admit that Wordsworth does divert energies of the Revolution into idealisms of art and nature, because he cannot face the complete moral assignment of that historical trauma (also personal trauma, since to himself he seems to have abandoned a lover and daughter who live in France). But in a famous 1980s attack on Wordsworth and Coleridge for fostering two centuries of bad faith and false consciousness, Jerome McGann in *The Romantic Ideology* (1983) may be displacing something too—an unadmitted preference for Byron, or an undeclared Marxism, or his own wish to be the herald of a postmodern poetics that cannot emerge without clearing the decks of the detritus of overvalued meditative writing.[4] For the other but not for oneself is thinking always ideological? The argument that Wordsworth did approach something like maximum possible consciousness, in and through his displacement into verbal art of the ideals of the French Revolution, plainly cannot be made if one cannot forgive his withdrawal, with most of the rest of the English nation, from the later stages of the 1789 Revolution. Who speaks, when, and from where? As Bakhtin always said, and says in the epigraphs above, point of view is literally everything.

My epigraphs come from Bakhtin's manuscript notes, written between the 1940s and the 1960s and published quite recently in the first volume (actually volume 5) of the multi-volume collected works (1996). These have appeared in a careful scholarly translation in an Italian literary journal, but have yet to appear in English. There are thirty-five pages of aphorisms and page-long statements that circle around certain insistences, already explained in previous commentary and in the present book. Here in the last chapter, it speaks to the coherence of Bakhtin's thought that the categories I developed as central for poetry in chapter 1—speaking subject, clash of inner and outer speech, intonation, image of a language—are all clustered and reexplained in valuable phrasing on several contiguous pages of these "Notes from the years 1940–1960." There are excellent pages on lying as "the most modern and topical form of evil" (50), which fill a gap in this writer's ethical system; and on love, about which Bakhtin says, "Only love can see and represent the interior liberty of the object" (46). Here, too, Bakhtin repeats his point about the impossibility of empty character zones, which is a reverse way of insisting that persons and utterances require each other: "a discourse of a nobody cannot exist" (55). In elaborating these familiar points, Bakhtin keeps returning to his most basic spatial image of alterity—physical distance as the precondition of knowing; physical distance as the guise of distance between persons, perspectives, eras. One note concerns a person in front of a mirror: "I have no point of view on my self from the outside" (15); another concerns the artistic imagination of a human being, the human's "forms and confines. The outline and the horizon" (49); and another, not even a full grammatical sentence but a note to himself for later development: "The complex problem of organizing centers" (60). Bakhtin engages in these meditations on perspective not to prod himself into a despairing relativism about knowledge, but rather to keep himself open to alterity, which is the source of dialogue and of trust in a world outside the self: "Because this is the nature of the artistic image: we are in it and outside of it, we live in it from the inside and see it from the outside. In this double experience and vision is the essence of artistic knowledge: 'the other life is mine-not-mine.' . . . [T]he artist lives in the hero and outside of the hero and unites these two aspects in the superior unity of the image" (55). Now the image of a discourse, by the second epigraph's understanding of perspective, is not the same as the image of a speaking human being; plainly to pursue the image of a discourse, or a clash of discourses, is to take the road less traveled. So with support from Bakhtin we can here abjure, for the most part, speaking human beings with biographies, in order to show lines of division within the discourses of Romanticism and of present-day scholarly studies of Romanticism.

Although many studies in the last twenty years refer to Bakhtin, and a few organize all argument according to utterance and dialogue directly in Bakhtin's line, my account will show that this is a distinct subset of current work, and one that usually has other concerns than to show the social moorings of Romantic poetry. (By contrast, New Historicists in the line of McGann have focused on the moorings to the exclusion of many other things, including utterance and dialogue.) Work that uses Bakhtin's terminology is indeed one of the discourses in the current clash, and I begin and end my survey with it.

My portal to the survey is Graham Pechey's "Not the Novel: Bakhtin, Poetry, Truth, God" (1989; expanded 1993; republished 2001).[5] Like the present book, Pechey in his essay takes on the centrality of the novel in Bakhtin as a problem. He accepts that poetry is often monologic, but tries to find an ambiguity in Bakhtin's idea of the poetic, a possibility for poetic types other than lyric-I genres, like epic and parody: for Pechey, the generic anomaly opens things up and permits socio-political thinking. His main example is William Blake as a renegade, quasi-Romantic writer whose ironies and apostrophes in poems such as "The Tyger" open potential social languages—monologisms that have possible utopian dimensions. Pechey brings Blake and Bakhtin into dialogue with one another, and in the process says a few things about Romanticism's special discourses: "The later Bakhtin would doubtless ascribe this inwardly anti-lyrical lyric to the work of 'novelisation' in the late eighteenth and early nineteenth centuries, and we might add that the lineage thus begun issues in the poetry of the various European modernisms" (65). Blake's writing is a "powerful hybrid of allegory and parody" (74–75), and also a parody of allegory! "What then does this strong poetic dialogism offer that novelistic dialogism cannot?" (76). The answers are: Blake offers the apostrophic word, as a gesture to the world outside the poem and to history, and he restores prophecy to genres that seemed deathbound.

My own view is that Blake is not as anomalous in the post-1789 period as Pechey makes him appear, and several of Pechey's points on Blake would be appropriate to describe allusion and apostrophe in Wordsworth too—though resistance to "hierarchised authority" (78) is much clearer in Blake than in Wordsworth, indeed remains the issue to be debated in Wordsworth.[6] Pechey ends with a brief section on more proclamatory, thus less ironic, poetic genres in apartheid and post-apartheid South Africa, his homeland. He writes about songs of and for the nation, and for the nation that might be: "a culture breaking out of the grip of such narratives also needs friendly forms of authority. Myths, hymns, anthems, prophecies, proverbs" (82). This is the first example, because others in the survey can be measured against Pechey's Bakhtinian sense of social pertinence, when struggles of one discourse against another for dominance are also struggles of political, and also theological, commitment.

In the late twentieth century scholarly clash of discourses, each roughly fifteen-year-long generation of scholarship on Romanticism, each wave of concern that gets a label and becomes influential for a while until it is itself surpassed, sees intensely the deficiencies of the just-previous kind of criticism. Then it sets about vigorously to correct the mistakes and supply the omissions. Then it too becomes routine, accepted in its main outlines as a part of knowledge. The discourse becomes permanently available as a resource, but less and less doable as a methodology, because the major moves have all been made, or because weakness has shown up in the original premise, or because the next discourse has already become the focus of attention. Conflicts that seemed to be vital clashes of principle at a special moment of time, turn out to be nearly invisible, flattened over the long duration. If this is so for the history of criticism in our own era, it must also be so for the object of that criticism, Romantic poetry from 1789–1815. The story of such writings, in such eras, becomes a reconstruction of causes of conflict. Here the aim is to show what is typical, not make a complete description, so I shall tell the story with names of critics and their methods standing for discourses.

The base position is pre–World War I belletrism, unscholarly but in favor of Romanticism in its more watery forms: the love lyrics in Palgrave's *Golden Treasury*, Swinburne's delicious drone, early Yeats, decadence, the non-theoretical impressionistic criticism of Walter Raleigh and Sir Arthur Quiller-Couch. Against this T. S. Eliot in his critical essays constructed a classicizing Modernism, to promote Donne and the metaphysical poets, Dryden, hard Augustan competence that eschewed emotion. Eliot, who started these polemics in the 1920s, largely as a way to clear a path and build a readership for his own poems, had a central role in forming the New Critics' polite distaste for Romantic writing, after about 1940. Often the New Critics employed Romanticism in their construction of a theory, but as negative examples: Cleanth Brooks's reproaches against Wordsworth in an essay on irony and W. K. Wimsatt's casting of doubt upon a whole way of making images of nature by comparison with the images of the metaphysical poets.[7] The Romantic poets, particularly from the first generation but not any of the women (of whom, later here), were the most spectacular examples of the affective and intentional fallacies, and insofar as Longinus on the Sublime seemed to sponsor Romantic excess that exceptionally intelligent, rational ancient critic was an object of scorn and refutation. (Wonderful and exact textual scholars who had no such bias flourished as contemporaries with, but outside, the later phases of the New Criticism, and among this group I would name Richard Harter Fogle, Walter Jackson Bate, Earl Wasserman, and David Perkins.) As New Criticism phases out in the late 1960s, a splendidly contentious era arrives with a far higher valuation of individual Romantic poets and of Romanticism as a movement. Now each method that arrives on the scene is preternaturally good at showing a neglected or new dimension of Romanticism, and at arguing for its importance.

With their interest in the poem itself, that mythical uninfluenced ideal, the New Critics were not inclined to read widely in philosophy or history. Those who nudged them off the scene in the late 1960s were what I will call consciousness critics, who were trained in Continental philosophy and eager to make comparisons between the English poets and such thinkers as Rousseau and Kant. Consciousness criticism in M. H. Abrams, Geoffrey Hartman, Harold Bloom, Paul De Man, and others took as its mission to add epistemology and ontology to New Critical premises, and as they did this, the quantity of textual analysis declined. They valued Romanticism for the kinds of philosophical thinking that New Criticism complained about, on psychological states, consciousness, anti-self-consciousness, personal growth, mind and world, the concept of nature, poetry as art. It turned out that these male poets—Wordsworth, Coleridge, Byron, Shelley, Keats—were all profound thinkers, making philosophy in poems, and also in their letters and essays contributing to the history of criticism.[8]

The leading alternative to consciousness criticism was and remains New Historicism, taking its origins and name from a small insurgent set of scholars of the English Renaissance, influenced by Michel Foucault and others to open a historical archive, a wide surround to imaginative writing in many other discourses, medical, juridical, and so on. In the writings of Stephen Greenblatt, Louis Montrose, Don E. Wayne, and others, imaginative writing was on the level with other writings in the archive, and instead of the retrospective term Renaissance they preferred Early Modern, which points forward. For them the breaking point in English literary history is the period of Shakespeare and Elizabeth I, which inaugurates acquisitive individualism, mercantilism, colonialism, and a new era of activist monarchs intelligent enough to rule through publicity including plays in public playhouses. When this historicist thinking, hyperaware of the position of the late-twentieth-century scholar as framing the position of the Early Modern writer, is in the mid 1980s brought over to the Romantic era in McGann and others, the new and lesser breaking point in the development of capitalism is the French Revolution. For McGann, Marjorie Levinson, Alan Liu, and others, many lines of theory converge on the Revolution, as a signal chance for literature to ally itself with progressive social change. When poets of the period fail to keep the faith in those ideals, their many modes of defection make the plots of articles and books. These scholars see Wordsworth and Coleridge, in particular, as writers who use nature, imagination, and narrative to transform into aesthetic play urgent political assignments of the era, such as achievement of rights for workers and women, emancipation of slaves, political equality for all classes, and curtailment of arbitrary behavior of the state toward its citizens. So New Historicist scholars in their earliest and purest argument become the scourge of Romantic poetry and of consciousness criticism. They attack the poetry for being not only unhistorical—but also deceptive, by inventing poems and critical slogans (like Wordsworth's "real language of men" description of his intent, in his preface to *Lyrical Ballads*) that pretend to be progressive while actually reserving elitist intentions. Pursuing their own discoveries of defections and absences, the New Historicist commentators have no wish to rehearse what the consciousness critics have discovered about this body of writing, or even to refute it, but the effect is dismissal for being unhistorical. The detail they collect from canonical and also never-analyzed texts by major male writers, and from the historical record, is often energetic, driven as it is by the passion to show heroic geniuses as conservative ideologues. Always this fascinating detail is worth considering and debating; but the scholars' frequent turn to the argument about repressions and displacements, which are indulged by clever poets hiding their tracks, is worrying from a logical point of view: unquestionably evidences about omissions are weaker than positive evidences. For this reason more negative evidences are needed to gain probative value, which makes for a criticism largely based in attitudes of suspicion. Unlike the Early Modern historicists, those who deal with Romanticism are concerned to debunk the reputations of the writers they study.[9]

Coming to prominence slightly after the consciousness and historicist critics of the 1980s, but with greater staying power into the present day, are the feminist critics of Romanticism. The other recent discourses have changed the way we read and the way we think about what we read, but doing this, the feminists have also changed the way we teach this literary period; thus their discourse is the most influential. They have expanded the canon by adding women writers and women's genres, and required comparison of post-1789 male and female writers—a large assignment, hardly now begun in the classroom.[10] One of the earliest scholars in this line is Margaret Homans, who showed Wordsworth's arrogant treatment of his able sister Dorothy, who materially contributed to his writing and reputation; and Homans argued persuasively that by addressing Nature with the pronoun "She," Wordsworth and other Romantic writers logically excluded females from the sphere of art and writing.[11] In several influential articles and two books, Mary Jacobus wrote about gender and genre, finding in the male writers, especially Wordsworth, a repression of sexual difference.[12] John Barrell in 1988 wrote a stunning chapter to show Wordsworth's placement of his sister Dorothy in the "language of the sense" at the end of "Tintern Abbey," arguing this was a deliberate attempt to place all women outside the language of intellect and moral judgment.[13] In the same year, Anne K. Mellor edited *Romanticism and Feminism* (1988), a collection of essays that showed the range and quality of women's writing in the period, and the extent of patriarchal attitudes ("Silencing the Female" is the title of one section) in the male writing. Mellor's volume included Stuart Curran's "The I Altered," a survey of Romantic women's poetry with analysis to show the themes and explicit merits of Mary Robinson, Anna Barbauld, Hannah More, Jane Taylor, Ann Yearsley, and especially Charlotte Smith.[14] In the next decade, there quickly ensued the publication of no less than four anthologies of Romantic women poets, and the reprinting of whole volumes that had not been printed or read, much less taught, since the early nineteenth century.[15] In the 1990s, the ubiquitous Norton Anthology and the upstart Blackwell and Longmans anthologies printed significantly expanded selections from Romantic women poets, and this has begun to change the structure of undergraduate courses in the field. Feminist criticism in this line, including the introductions to the anthologies, wishes to promote the texts of the women writers and show their quality—their example of a women's art and different genres from the male art, their attention to women's lives, their larger political purposes in affiliating with the French Revolution, with the poor, with slaves, with nationalist aspirations in Ireland, Scotland, and Wales. This criticism is actively angry that earlier discourses, in all the types I have so far shown, have omitted important women writers and the female point of view. However, apparently feminists assume in the male writers a bias against gender-family-society-political concerns, and in this they seem to omit a good deal of evidence both biographical and textual. Nor are feminist critics made uneasy that the women writers are rarely interested in the philosophical topics and aesthetic theory that male figures have been celebrated for—with one exception, in Anne K. Mellor's notice that the women poets do not express any need for the elevation they could gain from the Sublime, that category where limits vanish and which is central in Wordsworth and Coleridge.[16]

Another discourse of this period is harder to place because, while it has several component sources, it has behind it only one critic who has developed through different stages in her career: Tilottama Rajan. She emerges from De Man and consciousness criticism, with strong continental affiliations in German philosophy in the period of Schiller, and in existential phenomenology and Sartre. The title of her first book, *Dark Interpreter: The Discourse of Romanticism* (1980), shows her explicitly to be a student of discourse on discourse. She sounds increasingly like a deconstructionist who is trying to historicize herself and her writing, moving into the question of how the reader processes Romantic texts and how the writer builds the reader into texts dialogically. Her astute essay of 1985, "Romanticism and the Death of Lyric Consciousness," shows how Wordsworth in the famous owl calling scene in *The Prelude,* book 5, by an "interweaving of lyrical and narrative discourse, transforms lyric from a monological to a dialogical form." I quote the final sentences of this essay, to show how many discourses are clashing and defining one another, in the work of a careful thinker in our period:

Before we conclude, . . . we must add that the paradoxical nature of Romantic discourse can also be formulated in another way, in terms of the

survival of the lyrical voice within forms that erode its autonomy. Both
the dismantling of the traditional equation between Romantic literature
and lyric consciousness, and the recognition that the lyric is made inter-
discursive—but not eliminated—are constitutive moments in our understanding of the ontopoetics of Romanticism. Something other than a
New Critical approach to Romantic literature has seemed appropriate,
because Romanticism sees the absorption of the centered self into larger
processes that operate through it and thus decenter its own discourse.
But equally, the survival of the lyrical voice testifies to an understanding
of the self that is not quite that of poststructuralism: an understanding
of the self as constituted by and not deconstructed by its differences
from itself.

This late in my exposition, I trust the reader will be able to give the
proper name, not De Man, that these splendid sentences imply.
There is no reference whatever to Mikhail Bakhtin in this essay of
1985, but Rajan's book of 1990, *The Supplement of Reading*, with only
two small footnotes to the Russian is clearly a social interpretation
of poetry in Bakhtin's line and with his terms.[17]

The study of English Romanticism that is sanctioned by Bakhtin's
dialogic theory is less influential than feminist discourse on the period, and less contentious than New Historicist discourse. The Bakhtin discourse has been an adjunct, helping arguments with sources
from elsewhere, mediating rather than provoking clashes—and giving a frame for the present survey, even as it exists within the frame.
There are several heteroglossia and dialect studies in articles; there
is a book by Ashton Nichols on how Wordsworth's self-presentation
produces "a complex, polyvocal, and dramatized autobiographer";
and there are three books (by Paul Magnuson, Gene W. Ruoff, and
Lucy Newlyn) that appeal to dialogism to show how Wordsworth and
Coleridge in the period 1798–1804 are writing poems that reply to
each other, in running debate.[18] The use of Bakhtin in these studies
is correct, but opportunistic and brief. Several other Romanticists
write as committed specialists, with Bakhtin's terms: I am thinking
of Graham Pechey on Blake, whose essay I discuss above, of Lynn
Pearce on John Clare, and especially of Don H. Bialostosky's two
books on Wordsworth. These scholars have insisted on reading
poems as dialogues and narratives, finding clashes of discourse
within and between Romantic writers—and in Bialostosky attempting to arrange symposia of critical opinions in order to arrange synthesis on a grand scale. Bialostosky's first book, *Making Tales* (1984),

accepts Bakhtin's valuation of narrative forms and studies the plots
of Wordsworth's poems up to about 1805, emphasizing the stories.
He speaks in this book of "rhythmic telling," with an emphasis on
the ballad tale and not on the lyric intent; thus he prevents himself
from seeing that the poems are also telling rhythm, which is my
point of correction against Bakhtin in chapter 4 of the present book.
Bialostosky's second book, *Wordsworth, Dialogics, and the Practice of
Criticism* (1992), takes the utterances of speaking subjects in lyrics
far more seriously: he sees the inability of consciousness and New
Criticisms to deal with persons in poems, and with utterance generally, and he tries to make himself more historical on the pattern of
the New Historicists. Of all the books listed in this chapter, this second of his books is the most capacious and judgmental survey of the
clash of discourses in our period; he restricts himself to Wordsworth
criticism, but covers all the discourses I have scanned, letting the
types talk to each other, and finding that only readings through the
lens of Bakhtin are fully attentive to utterances.[19] I conclude my own
symposium of clashing critical discourses by drawing forth a moral
from Bialostosky: being attentive to who is speaking and to whom,
the reader is attentive to persons in poems, and (within the art) this
is the start of all politics.

COMPARISON OF WOMEN'S AND MEN'S WRITING, 1789–1815

"The complex problem of organizing centers": Bakhtin's note,
cited in passing above, fits our own era's interpretation of Romanticism as sketched above; but the complexity grows exponentially
when we attempt to organize the clash of discourses in England after
1789. We must use our discourses to organize theirs, but ours are to
some extent determined by theirs—that is the point of McGann's
Romantic Ideology: his wish to cast off all determinants, or all that he
finds are merely ideologies that have come to seem natural. Mc-
Gann's polemic treatise has much to recommend it, as a method for
tracing the social moorings of poetry and poetics. What is social is
the ideological languages within national languages; what is social is
always a clash, which need not be destructive—rather dialogic, because those in dialogue are by definition not at war. Better to fight
it out on the territory of the utterance than on the battlefield or in
the civil war! To this kind of struggle, there is no end and no resolu-

tion. This very irresolution may cause Bakhtinian literary scholarship to part company, eventually, with McGann's Foucauldian social constructionism, where the organizing centers are small in number and crushing in power. Do social construction theories survive less well when the numbers of organizing centers are multiplied? Do social construction theories survive less well when the clashes are extensively mapped, all the way down to utterances and their internal and external divisions? Is it possible that writers of the early Romantic period, notably Wordsworth and Coleridge, have refuted in advance some of the critiques leveled at them by McGann and the New Historicists? When women writers are reckoned in to the array of discourses in our period, how does their presence change the pattern of divisions?

Literary scholarship could be a re-creation of a clash of discourses from an earlier period, or from the present day of the scholar-writer. That we have not taken this on as a normal task is due, I think, to our fascination with authors at the expense of discourses, and to our lack of organizing centers, or our naming of only one center as the full explanation. Turning now to a trial of method with the Romantic period itself, I propose a comparison of topics and texts, to show the clash of discourses within male and female poetry of the period: I am interested in the grounds of comparison that moor the male and the female poets to the typical concerns of their period, and that show their different accounts of experience and of verbal art. Admittedly a sketch, this is bound to be reliant on schemas, but has at least this merit: now that the women writers are within the canon, we owe it to their achievement to discuss them in the same lecture, course, and book with the better known male figures. If it is to be a true comparison, it will be inconvenient somewhere on all conceivable sides of the several organizing centers.

No easy oppositions, then, beginning with the opposition male/female: Anne K. Mellor is right to remind us that the women poets adapt male gestures and languages, including the rhetoric of the Sublime, and that the men do entertain the women poets' themes on occasion, including the vocabulary of feeling and communication. Still, as Mellor also says, in every opposition one side is always, if covertly, privileged, and the male side is privileged in the period 1789–1815. That is a given, and a condition of possibility that constrains all of social and literary life.[20]

My array of comparison topics for women's and men's writing

ranges widely across seven discourses in the period 1789–1815—widely but thinly, with evidences mostly from impressions gathered from my own reading. I will not perform the comparisons, but only offer hints about which directions might be productive; this prepares for my account of divisions in an eighth discourse, on slavery in contemporary poems by Amelia Opie and William Wordsworth.

Favored Words

The diction of a period is one clue to typical norms and concerns.

Using the Duncan Wu anthology, (*Romantic Women Writers* 1997), as my textual base, I judge that the favored, recurrent words of the women are: soft, gentle, nature, genius, female, angel, fancy, freedom, sorrow, horror, and pant (as a verb).

Using Josephine Miles's word lists for Wordsworth only, I judge that the favored words of one leading male poet are: feelings, nature, love, tree, mountain, hate, fear, passion, affection, tears, laughter, emotion, pleasure, joy, grief, happy, pride, man, life, delight, power, and heart.[21]

This is the weakest kind of evidence, and (though logical) the most minimal beginning.

Favored Genres

In the women poets favored genres are: story poems, poems addressed to other women, poems on/to places, ballads, sonnets (Charlotte Smith in particular), satire (Joanna Baillie), and thoughts at the grave of a poetess.

In Wordsworth and Coleridge they are: odes, ballads, autobiographical blank verse, supernatural poems (Coleridge), sonnets (Wordsworth), poems with dates in their titles, "effusions," and sublime landscape poems.

Favored Themes

In the women poets: the definition of sensibility, family, social life, women and women writers, the poor, London, the Lake District, and apostrophe to male writers.

In Wordsworth and Coleridge: walking, places, excursion into the world, children and innocence, being surprised into a perception, birds, flowers, public pronouncement, country people, and property.

Relation to Women's Experience

In the women poets: defense of women's minds and equality, portrayal of female black slaves in the colonies, education of girls, the English woman, different experiences of women in lower and upper classes, and warnings against male predators. (There is here a notable absence of poems on love and falling in love.)

In Wordsworth and Coleridge: obsession with women who have lost their children (as in Wordsworth's "The Thorn"), dead little girls, betrayed innocence (as in Coleridge's "Christabel"), and praise of women poets. (There are few grown women in Wordsworth and Coleridge; and there remains the disturbing question of Wordsworth's treatment of his sister's journals, taking her ideas and phrasing for his own poems.)

Relation to Language

In the women poets: language as a public instrument, belief in logic and clarity, the need for rhyme and meter to signify poetry, and minor use of dialect (Joanna Baillie, Amelia Opie).

In Wordsworth and Coleridge: a language within public language—the avant-garde intention, struggle for meaning, Wordsworth's language of interfusion of mind and world; "Form as Proceeding" in Coleridge—aesthetics of process in creation, controversy over the "real language of men" and whether it may exist in poetry, and Wordsworth's consignment of sister Dorothy and all women and children to the "language of the sense," less intellectual than the language of the mind. (The male writers make large contributions to the theory of poetic language.)

Relation to the Sublime and to Imagination

In the women poets: Charlotte Smith refers to the landscape sublime at the beginning and end of her excellent meditative poem, "Beachy Head," and Letitia Elizabeth Landon pays attention to artistic improvisation in her poem "The Improvisatrice." But where "imagination" is a topic in the earlier group of writers like Anna

Laetitia Barbauld and Hannah More, it is a dangerous or misleading force; for them the preferred term is "fancy." It is still a matter of debate whether there can be such a thing as a domestic Sublime in the women poets, as Anne K. Mellor has argued—Since the sublime is in Longinus-Burke-Kant traditionally the exceeding of the domestic, and of thresholds of any sort.

In Wordsworth and Coleridge: the Sublime of mountains and the imagination that confronts it are central to their thought—to Wordsworth's obsession with death and eternity, and to Coleridge's metaphysical belief in the "one life" within the human being and abroad. Fear is the keynote in Wordsworth's "Spots of Time" in *The Prelude*. Between them, these two writers are the primary forces in placing these terms in the forefront of intellectual history, for their era and the whole of the nineteenth century.

Relation to the French Revolution

In the women poets: From 1789 to 1793, Seward, Smith, Yearsley, and Williams all write important poems on the Revolution, affiliating with it and hoping it will cross the Channel to England. In poems written after 1793, the women poets express some worries about king-killing and violence.

In Wordsworth and Coleridge: After an initial euphoric stage of pro-French sentiment, where they think of the Revolution as the dawn of a new human society, both the male poets withdraw from their earlier positions: an avoidance and driving-inward of the political. Wordsworth has what amounts to a breakdown where, he says, he yields up moral questions in despair; and Coleridge by stages becomes a Tory apologist. The plot of deconversion, defection, and displacement into aesthetic activity is favored by most interpreters of their lives and writings, but is that the whole story?

Relation to Slavery and to the Abolitionist Movement after 1789

In the women poets: The Duncan Wu anthology has ten long, eloquent poems about slavery by poets from Hannah More in 1788 to Isabella Lickbarrow in 1814. Some of these are historical and statemental, and some are enactive story-poems. Very frequently the women poets present the scene of physical torture, or of family disruption, as a way to rouse the reader to identify with the lives, the very sensations of slaves. The writers are all intelligent agents of abolitionist thought, and show awareness of being part of a social movement against deeply entrenched power.

In Wordsworth: The poet in book 10 of *The Prelude* devotes about forty lines to show his early knowledge of the discourse of abolitionism. When he was in London in the early 1790s, he says, there was a "strong levy of humanity / Upon the traffickers in Negro blood" (lines 248–49), but he gave little attention to this, assuming that when the government changed, state-sponsored slaveholding "Would fall together with its parent tree" (line 262).[22] However, when the poet was in France in 1790, a bill to prohibit slave trading under the British flag passed in the Commons but failed in the Lords (such a bill passed only much later, in 1807); this was the first "shock" to Wordsworth's "moral nature" (lines 268–69), and it made him feel shame for England. He appears to say that this politicized him—leaving him unsettled about his country's role until February 1793 when France declared war on England and Holland, thus pulling him back to patriotic feelings. So his allegiances were confused by far-off historical events he could not control. First drafted in 1805 to rescue a time of uncertainty, this text may contain Wordsworth's one memory of the discourse on slavery; here, the politics of slavery is an early stage in his psychological crisis. There is one other text on slavery: writing in 1802 when he has come out the other side of his political-moral crisis, and when he feels able to pronounce on slavery, he speaks directly "To Toussaint L'Ouverture"—to a former slave turned master, now in a prison in Paris.

I shall compare Wordsworth's famous political sonnet of 1802 with Amelia Opie's long story-poem published the same year, "The Negro Boy's Tale." We do not know if they knew each other's work, but these are two entirely admirable contemporary poems on the same topic, and we may conduct from our vantage the clash of discourses. It is an especially revealing clash because the female and male discourses divide within the larger shared language of abolitionist politics. The four categories for comparison are those I drew together in chapter 1, from scattered places in Bakhtin.

Opie's story poem is in ballad quatrains: Zambo has been stolen from his home in Africa to work as a plantation slave in Jamaica, British territory.[23] Trevannion is the captain of a British ship ready to leave the island, but now (lines 1–15) his daughter Anna cannot be found because she is listening to Zambo's story in his own words—so we have first person speech in Jamaican English from line 16 to line 88, an unusual *tour de force*, subject to all the commentary on the social poetics of dialect brought forward in chapter 2 above. Will Zambo be allowed to sail to England or Africa? He dreams of it:

> 'Missa', poor Zambo cried, 'sweet land
> Dey tell me dat you go to see,
> Vere, soon as on de shore he stand,
> De helpless negro shall be free.
>
> 'Ah, dearest missa, you so kind!
> Do take me to dat blessed shore,
> Dat I mine own dear land may find,
> And dose who love me see once more.
>
> 'Oh, ven no slave, a boat I buy,
> For me a letel boat vould do,
> And over wave again I fly,
> Mine own loved negro land to view.'

(lines 16–28)

In Zambo's dialect voice, Amelia Opie conveys the pain of his parting from his mother in Africa, "De heavy chain my body bear," the crowding and the "sick air" on the boat across the Atlantic, the slave's sense of inner worth and his wish to board the ship with Anna. But Anna boards alone with her father, and Zambo is left behind:

> Meanwhile, poor Zambo's cries to still,
> And his indignant grief to tame,
> Eager to act his brutal will,
> The negro's scourge-armed ruler came.
>
> The whip is raised, the lash descends,
> And Anna hears the sufferer's groan;
> But while the air with shrieks she rends,
> The signal's given—the ship sails on.

(lines 137–44)

Zambo swims after the ship and is drowned. In the last sixteen lines Opie speaks in her own voice, no longer a storytelling voice but a mourning and pitying one for the "countless Zambos" who are oppressed from Ceylon and India to Jamaica. She ends by invoking a force that may seem external, but emerges from the best human impulses:

> Come Justice, come, in glory dressed,
> Oh come, the woe-worn negro's friend,
> The fiend-delighting trade arrest,
> The negro's chains asunder rend!

(lines 185–88)

The discourse of Justice applies to all persons, regardless of skin color or place of birth.

Wordsworth's sonnet "To Toussaint L'Ouverture" is better known, but it is not known in this contrastive pairing with Opie's poem of story, dialect speech, and protest:

> Toussaint, the most unhappy man of men!
> Whether the whistling Rustic tend his plough
> Within thy hearing, or thy head be now
> Pillowed in some deep dungeon's earless den;—
> O miserable Chieftain! where and when
> Wilt thou find patience? Yet die not: do thou
> Wear rather in thy bonds a cheerful brow:
> Though fallen thyself, never to rise again,
> Live, and take comfort. Thou hast left behind
> Powers that will work for thee: air, earth, and skies;
> There's not a breathing of the common wind
> That will forget thee; thou hast great allies;
> Thy friends are exultations, agonies,
> And love, and man's unconquerable mind.

Toussaint stood against the slavery and colonialism of France, and has been brought from margin to metropole of empire, to be imprisoned: that it is the evil of France, country of Wordsworth's English enemy, may free Wordsworth to protest injustice; though "air, earth, and skies," and the end of the poem show that he knows evil easily crosses international borders.

The Speaking Subject in Opie and Wordsworth

The genre in Opie's poem is the tale, and the point of view for telling is omniscient—or seems to be all-knowing and impersonal at the middle-of-the-action opening lines. There are many changes of speaker, in this order: Trevannion, omniscient author, Zambo in dialect, omniscient author, Zambo and Anna in dialogue, omniscient, Trevannion, omniscient, Anna, Trevannion, and last, the authorial I. Quick, dramatic change of speaking subject is the method of telling, but the poem does, in retrospect, funnel toward its personal-polemical final lines that point a moral basing the conclusion on the example of the dramatic opening and middle moves.

Wordsworth's is a lyric speaking subject: himself as author in the first person, speaking to an absent addressee, Toussaint, the Haitian slave-emperor. He sympathizes with the black revolutionary, and offers support through sympathy for prison life, through injunctions, and through lists of allies. His fourteen-line poem is equivalent in speaking subject and political intent to the final sixteen lines of Opie's text, but lacks Opie's previous tale with its narrative drive and its many changes of speaker. By contrast, Opie's text does not have direct authorial address to the black slave, but gains remarkable moral force by letting the slave speak at length, so that the reader hears about injustice in the victim's very words; those words are imaginary, ventriloquial, and put into dialect in formal quatrains, but the reader accepts the artifice.

The Clash of Inner and Outer Speech in Opie and Wordsworth

In the tale of Zambo, there is a heavy presentation of outer speech—in the inner tale itself in dialect, but also in the unpredictable shift of speakers once Zambo has finished his long story. Inner speech is important, as I have hinted, when the poem's intent is political conversion: when we get a slave's experience in a slave's voice and dialect, the details may be sentimental, but the force of the utterance will be taken more directly to the reader's sympathies. At the end, the pose of objectivity must slip, and the female author emerges as an I in the present tense: the author speaks to the created character when she says, "Anna, I mourn thy virtuous woe. . . ." (line 173), and when she calls on a personified Justice to free a whole race. The tale, as genre, seems remarkably flexible to permit movement from outer to inner speech, and equally from inner to outer: as much a persuasive transition as a clash of discourses.

Wordsworth in his poem manages to be public as well as intimate—intimate leading to public forms of address, widening the context even as the addressee remains constant. The address is personal, but the intent is to turn utterance toward a universal value of freedom: even Nature, the earth itself, is against slavery and French colonialism! At this level of energetic abstraction, where *wind* and *mind,* and *skies* and *allies,* may rhyme together the natural and the human, inner speech transforms into outer speech with no sense of a clash. A 2002 dissenting voice will complain that the clash of inner and outer speech is finessed by Wordsworth's idealism, operating through assertions in the diction and the formal properties of the poem. This I accept: plainly author and poem flaunt their idealism, with no apology for antislavery politics.

Intonation in Opie and Wordsworth

Intonation is the display of social tones in the text, and in Opie this is conveyed through the simple quatrain stanza that carries the tale and helps blend in the concluding polemic; through the profusion of adjectives that cue the reader's response to kidnapping and torture in slavery; and through details of the story in Zambo's own voice, whose dialect is there to break the reader's heart. In Opie, genre and speaking subject direct the changes of intonation. We have a change of the omniscient author into a speaker, and accordingly intonation changes from sentimental tale to idealistic plea. Her poem's opening is into vigorous action of plot, and her ending rises into noble abstraction.

Social tones in Wordsworth's poem move from apostrophe, to questioning gestures, to commands, to grand and spacious description in the lists of the final six lines. This is a sequence of increasingly social tones, a crescendo of idealism and general relevance. Even the lists at the end are in dramatic sequence, from the natural forces ranged against slavery, to violent and loving human forces—the emotional and the cognitive working together.

The Image of a Language in Opie and Wordsworth

Both Opie and Wordsworth imagine a transnational image of a language, because any discourse that will defeat the international discourse (and fact) of slavery must match the opponent in flexibility and generality.

Bakhtin would call Opie's poem "novelized" because of its extended plot and its play with changing speakers. This is narrative language and method, with a personal-polemical curl at the end. Opie's main innovation to extend beyond conventional images of poetic language is the daring use of Black dialect. Perhaps the dialect section is only partly successful as orthography but certainly does quickly carry the reader into the experience of the slave. Opie's genre and method require a realist image of language: her ballad stanza, overall tale-telling intent, and skill in switching viewpoints with speakers, reinforce her use of several identifiable sociolects, all English, all pointing in the direction of an abolitionist global politics.

Wordsworth's text points in the same direction, but his language is more mandarin (nowhere more so than at "unconquerable"!) as he skirts realism in the octave, then leaves it in the sestet. The account of Powers from line 10 to the end is huge in scope; this is a language that can show the outer world in sympathy with humanity's best universal impulses. There is a considerable reach, from exultations to agonies to love to man's mind. In this language, the physical is the intellectual and can convert monologue to intimate dialogue over the distance from England to France, and in the short space of fourteen lines. Almost, the formality of the sonnet structure disappears in the generation of this claim for a boundary-destroying natural language.

The two poems contain personal speech from the identifiable author, but very differently framed. One is a rather long tale, and one is a brief lyric; one invents a dialect speech, and one finds (through direct address to a named historical person) a way to be energetic about Enlightenment generalities concerning freedom. Wordsworth reckons the natural world into the struggle for justice, and Opie appeals directly to the personified ideal of Justice. There is no need to make a decision about which is the more effective method. Nor, despite the sexism of "man's unconquerable mind," do we need to identify one method as exclusively a woman's method. The discourses may indeed clash, but here the political goal is shared—denunciation of slavery as the tentacle of a reigning monologic discourse of power, which would never care to moor itself in poetry, or any other public form of utterance.

CLASH OF DISCOURSES IN THE AMERICAN 1990S: ROBERT PINSKY AND CHARLES BERNSTEIN

Thus Romanticism, and its presence in current scholarship. If we turn the telescope around upon ourselves, we may perhaps confirm that the heritage of Romanticism is still with us, enabling, disabling. Many indeed have argued a curious arc back from the postmodern, which was joyfully proposed twenty years ago as the final surpassing of Romantic premises, to certain vital strains in Romanticism.[24] Briefly now as a closing instance of the clash of discourses, I would isolate two types of writing in American poetry of the 1990s. One way to define the clash is as a matter of tendency—against or for a line of affiliation back to Romantic premises and achievement. "Against a line of affiliation" is very likely too mild a way to put the negative side of this because those who resist what they consider the false Romantic recoil from it in disgust. Narrowing the issue for the sake of provocation, let us call this a clash over *personal voice* in writing. The line between personal and textual voice in writing is often overridden in both directions, but still the line exists and the personal side has ancient, contorted roots in Romanticism and Whitman. The question has some pertinence in a book that proposes Bakhtinian types of reading, because Bakhtin, while he several times downgraded poetry as monologic (meaning, here, overpersonal), was also unable to acknowledge that such a thing as textual voice was possible in literature. In the clash of discourses I am constructing in American poetry of the most recent past, Bakhtin was unsympathetic to both types. But for him they were different: though personal voice he thought too limited, he never acknowledged the existence of textual voice.[25]

The American 1990s began in 1989, in Russia and eastern Europe in the collapse of communism, and in the 1991 Gulf War. Then ensued the election of Bill Clinton and the collapse of his plan for a redesign of the American health care system, legislation to end the failed structure of Welfare by requiring work and adding term limits, the disasters of Somalia, Bosnia and Rwanda, the coming of NAFTA and the rescue of the Mexican economy, the sexual and impeachment scandals of the Clinton era, the surprise of the dot.com economy that floated enormous successes in the stock market to the end of the decade, the protection of Kosovo against Serbia and the bombing of Belgrade, the disputed election of George W. Bush, and many other world-historical events. This decade, defined as an era of dominant themes and feelingtone, found its emphatic end in the terrorist attacks on the World Trade Towers and the Pentagon on September 11, 2001. American poetry in this decade, including the work of my two chosen writers—Charles Bernstein and Robert Pinsky—made some show of referring to history, but gave remarkably little attention to the events just listed. In the poetry world the 1990s produced a number of disparate emergent events, including for example the new popularity of competitive poetry slams where the audience voted to decide which of several poets was the most appealing; the proliferation of contests for new poets set up by university presses and poetry journals, where writers sent in manuscripts plus twenty dollars to be judged by anonymous experts and possibly published but usually rejected; the coming to prominence of greater numbers of African- and Asian- and Native-American and Chicano poets, male and female, and also of proudly gay or lesbian poets; the continuing restraining traditional presence of the American Academy of Poets and of *Poetry* magazine; the solidification of the insurgent Language Poets by big press publication, by their winning prestige teaching posts in American universities, by books and articles on them and by their own publishing of works of theory. In 2000 was published Cary Nelson's *Anthology of Modern American Poetry*, which I will use as a symposium of the whole era: admirable full selections from Whitman, Dickinson, Stevens, Eliot, Moore, and other well known modernists, with a revisionary wide selection from the thirties including women, working class, and African-American writers and notably the admirable work of the early Muriel Rukeyser; with Japanese American Concentration Camp Haiku, 1942–44; with a decent selection from the late modernists who emerged after 1945, especially ample from Robert Lowell and Frank O'Hara; and ending in the last 220 pages (of 1222) with a Wide ranging set of imaginative selections from younger poets (born after 1940) of many different kinds—Yusef Komunyakaa, C. D. Wright, Ron Silliman, Sandra Cisneros, Marilyn Chin, Susan Howe, Sherman Alexie, to name several. Nelson keeps but sifts writers of the past, brings forward neglected figures on grounds both social and poetic—also experimental writers, a category usually avoided—and he is a recognizer of promising talent.[26] In the late 1990s, our two chosen poets both had public roles: Robert Pinsky was Poet Laureate for several years and appeared regularly with poetry talks on a national news program on public broadcasting television, and Charles Bernstein appeared, backed by books in his office and making jokes, in a puckish television advertisement for the phone company's Yellow Pages. Pinsky is anthologized in the Nelson anthology, with two poems of strong social relevance on the Holocaust and on sweatshop labor, but Bernstein is not in Nelson. In this comparison of very recent books, Pinsky's *Jersey Rain* is published by the prominent commercial house, Farrar, Straus and Giroux, and Bernstein's *With Strings* is with distinguished company in the poetry series at University of Chicago Press.[27] Pinsky, the translator of Dante's *Inferno*, dedicates his book to Louise Gluck and Stephen Greenblatt, two establishment figures; by contrast, Bernstein has a twelfth-century epigraph in his book from Girault de Bornelh to make a policy statement that "sense remote / Adduces worth," and he refers in his notes at the end to avant-garde writers Douglas Messerli and Nicole Brossard. In the contrast that follows, each poem must stand for a book and each book for a number of similar writers and books. The poets are so markedly different, it is hard to imagine that they are both Americans roughly similar in age and equal in reputation; and, though representative, these are but two of the many types one might identify among the discourses in the final pages of the Nelson anthology, from poets born after 1940.

As a hint of the disparity that makes for dramatic contrast, there are in these books no two poems on a similar theme. A minor comparison first: Pinsky's title poem "Jersey Rain" (52) is the last in his book, and seems to be a match with Bernstein's uncapitalized title, "ruminative ablution" (71). Where Pinsky would say *rain*, Bernstein would say *ablution*; where Pinsky would justify his title by the whole poem, Bernstein would disconnect title from poem; where Pinsky would typically begin with a question to himself to energize his utterance, Bernstein would begin with a pun involving a sorry mispronunciation ("I've got a hang for *langue*") and a quick unexplained reference to Ferdinand de Saussure's langue-parole distinction; where Pinsky would produce a line of images showing the rain's opposed qualities ("source of art and woe") and the places it falls ("Metuchen, Rahway, Saddle River," and four other named towns), Bernstein would sentence by sentence work through references to an egg cream, "each to his own goo" (punning on French *goût*), licking stamps, a Honolulu sunset, a slice of cheese, Worcestershire sauce, "sauce for the gander," and a turn to an unidentified "you" to recommend "if you can't buy / Redemption" then lease it (here a buried reference to Green Stamps, which I believe are no longer current, but they used to be "redeemed"). Here, Bernstein's several rhymes are encountered as instances in unpredictable mid-line places, but Pinsky's rhymes fall by formal design, in the usual alternating end-line places in traditional quatrains. If both poems are, to use Bernstein's term, "ruminative," then Bernstein's is a comedic hop-skip-jump of ratiocination, with sentences seemingly unrelated to one another and ending on a question, and Pinsky's is a heavily orchestrated waltz ending on a plangent affirmation (Jersey rain as paradoxically "executioner, [and] source of life").

A more revealing contrast is between two longer, non-lyric programmatic poems, which use their sequence of images to make an argument. Both are three pages long; both are meditations on the meaning of meaning, but only Pinsky is traditional enough to rely on a genre term in his title, "Ode to Meaning," and only Pinsky maintains a consistent pose of address to this personified concept. Bernstein's title, working heavily his preference for prefixes and suffixes, and his satire-by-overuse of academic language, is "besotted desquamation."

Pinsky in his free verse Ode says he is "untrusting" but nonetheless he "court[s]" meaning, and the poem tosses up several convergent images to pin down, or at least salute, elusive meaning. So in his more relaxed formal choices and in his stance, he is here closer than anywhere in his book to Bernstein's more thoroughgoing, philosophically based skepticism about how we know through language. Indeed near the end he seems to have Bernstein in mind when he says to meaning, his addressee, "Let those scorn you who never / Starved in your dearth." To take this as a bitter dialogue is of course the critic's construct, but any reader will here remember this book's five separate, agonized references to Pinsky's mother's concussion, which forever harmed her and their family (six lines on this topic in this poem). For Pinsky, meaning is dire but desired, a cleavage but also a stirring, a wound but also medicine—and so on, through similes and oppositions to convey the difficulty of making sense, the value of irresolution. Although he attends to the negative, plainly his discourse (as in that early social-erotic reference to courting meaning) enjoys the hunt, finds meaning everywhere, and (as in the last-page, capitalized reference to "Imagination") trusts the writer to concentrate what sense there is to be won from the world. The pronoun "You" appears twenty times; despite his disclaimers, so much does he possess the trust of a Romantic heritage that he can address meaning directly like a person, for the length of the poem. For this writer, the social moorings of poetry are to be found in its ability to process disparate information over a wide range of experience, and to constellate meaning-as-rhythm.

Meaning is derailed from the very opening at Bernstein's title, because a "besotted desquamation," or drunken taking-off of scales, does not easily compute with the poem, and there is a chance that its role is to explode the space, and use, of titles generally, by pompous nonsense. But in a writing that de-tones itself, how does the reader know where nonsense is deliberate? It is possible that each of the five hundred or so alliterative words, each of the one hundred lines, or each alphabetical letter that structures the overall series of this poem, is a scale to be stripped off by uttering it in an unexpected or non-rational ("besotted") order. But how validate that guess, and how narrow to which of these is the scale that is . . . meant? When there is obscurity built into the design, and when social tones are omitted or parodied, the reader has unusually heavy assignments. Being forced to do the hard work is only fair, but it may be necessary even in the avant-garde text to offer the lure of an array of plausible hypotheses on authorial intent. Is that likely, if meaning as category in and around the words is undermined? Can there be social moorings for poetry if the lines are de-toned and meanings multiplied or apparently deferred?

Bernstein in this poem uses the alphabet, slightly scrambled because he begins with S, M, and L before doubling back to A, as a spine for a plot made up of one-line units, lines which are themselves four or five words long, and structured by ancient alliterative method, thus: "Moored by mutilated mink martinis" (line 10). Each line's sequence of images is arbitrary along the plot dictated by the first letters of words, on the showing of this example; and so too, apparently, the linkage between the separate lines, along the hoax plot dictated by verbs of action; and the sequence of the alphabet, framing the whole but playfully rearranged, is the meaning of relationships in a dictionary not those of a natural-language utterance, or a story. The story is in the denial of story, and of meaning—and beyond that, in the amazing human ability to make sectors of meaning out of hints aleatory or deranged. The voice produced is what I call textual voice, because of the deliberate exclusion of biographical speaking; this is the performance voice of an intellectual comedian who would rigorously exclude from the discourse all idealisms of imagination, person, truth, logic, narrative, and the structure of the English sentence. Such a voice dares to seem ugly, obscure, and self-involved because always drawing attention to metaphors of writing in the midst of writing; but wisely, this textual voice does not prolong the performance to the point of seeming also tedious. For Bernstein, the social moorings of poetry are to be found in its ability to disrupt known plots and to blow away, through laughter, anything that looks like an essence; Bernstein is moored by mutilated mink martinis. However it is clear from his "notes and acknowledgements" at the end of the book that he considers his work in the first instance political and social.

Vocabularies in themselves, before syntax, may suggest a relation to Romantic tenets. In Robert Pinsky's book overall, his recurrent or typical words are *civic, mother, imagination, presence, soul, alphabet, congeries, spandrel, crappy, perfect, eloquence, mastery, liquefaction, life.* Bernstein's words are *autarkic, structurelessness, mickey mousing, cockamamie, speechlessness, simulation, a dollop of hokum, suturing chiasma, gelatinous shrues, defenestrated micropassage, bumbling, truesome.* Pinsky is quite willing to write in his own first person, but in Bernstein, the upright pronoun is so often an absence or an invented other ("I am not I" [50]; "erasure me" [45]), we cannot know exactly when he is claiming it for himself. Aristotle spoke of the need for a mixed diction, drawn from several places and professions, and Bernstein must be one of the most mixed of all who now write. Bernstein is willing to put interjections and neologisms into the middle of high-art talk, mixing *uh, er, guys* with *preemptory perforation,* and mixing references to Cratylus with children's language and rhymes. Both Pinsky and Bernstein show parodic contempt for advertising language and certain kinds of debased popular culture. But Bernstein's range of vocabularies and jostling discourses is immensely wider—in one book, ad-speak, child-speak, street-speak, academic lingo-speak, tough guy-speak, freak-speak, capitalist-speak, Wallace Stevens-speak, Emily Dickinson-speak, and no doubt others. There is not a pun or a homophony or a chance thought Bernstein will reject, or a cliché he can resist reversing. For someone who seems willing to let waves of language wash over him, unlike Pinsky who fends off much that is horrid or inconvenient, Bernstein is prone to making things happen by verbs of command, and by the fiats of impossible narrative. In Bernstein, things happen in and by language because reference and person are so doubtful; in Pinsky, things happen in the ordinary world of families, politics, and objects, which he trusts and hopes to meliorate; this is why he makes so much of civic virtues, "civic art"

(42) in four of his poems. This is also why he still seems to credit the Romantic linkage that Bernstein so vigorously resists—the line that runs spirit-air-breath-voice-eloquence-song-poetry.

Neither of these writers, the one who loves perfection and the one who loves its opposites, emerges from the contrast with undiminished credit. Robert Pinsky organizes his book by several key themes—family, the civic, remembrance, the concentrated re-presentations of art, and some others—and he has an engaging habit of linking one poem thematically with the just-following one, in continuing chains of topics. Low-key elegance and eloquence are his signature qualities, but he repeats some awkward gestures: beginning poems with rhetorical questions to get himself going, ending poems with slightly too marmoreal truths and the too efficient meshing of easy rhymes. There is one awful poem, his least controlled and his longest: "An Alphabet of My Dead," whose embarrassing alpha-list of dead persons is brilliantly contravened by Charles Bernstein's rigorous use of a similar method, described above. Bernstein claims in his concluding notes that *With Strings* is full of echoes and recurrences of words, ideas; that is indeed the meaning of his title— strings of meanings organize the book as a whole, even as meaning is dubious in any local moment. With a Ph.D. and fifty years of practice and four readings of the book, this reader cannot identify many of these lines of logic, so I take the author's claim on trust. Strings, very likely, are lines of words that are put together with some randomness, to let the meanings collide and reunite if they can. Bernstein requires continual reconceptualization because of the "tears" and "leaks" of language (119, 97), but he still proposes late in the book the command, school policy of all those who call themselves language writers, "let language lead." On this logic, if the writer follows where language leads, he or she will escape domination by the Romantic essences that push and pull language from the outside. However, thus to decertify the writer's own prowess might be a way to call greater attention to it, as the writer performs antics and ugliness *with no constraint from public meanings*, no requirement to produce recognizable tones of voice. I admire Bernstein most on his very last page, where in fifty or so lines beginning "I / know that the radiance before me has no / name," (128) he gets down off the comedian's stage and speaks in what is apparently his own name in long tough elegiac lines, still honorably anti-Romantic but with uncharacteristic steely sobriety.

As I have already quoted Bakhtin as saying: "The complex problem of organizing centers." Coming from different universes of discourse, these two writers seem to relate to each other as counterparts, seem often to be actively refuting each other, denying each other public space. This is the guess of the person outside their clashing American languages, who might have the brief illusion, that in some other chronotope these writers would together make a language more whole, more moored to American society. But there is no other chronotope than the time/space contemporary critics and writers inhabit, and one way to define its particularity and imagine something other is to map the clash of discourses.

Afterword: One More Thing
I Know about Bakhtin

ALTHOUGH MIKHAIL BAKHTIN HAS BEEN UNDERSTOOD AS AN EXAMPLE and sponsor for Marxist-liberationist readings, there is no strong evidence that he is consciously consistently a Marxist thinker. Although Bakhtin has been taken, wrongly, as an example and sponsor for Formalist readings, there is plenty of evidence that he is an opponent of Russian Formalism even as he respects the Formalist achievement in the twenties. In his relationship to these literary approaches that seem to stand for worldviews, it is not a matter of either-or, or of neither-nor; and it is not a matter of his being someplace between the two approaches. *Where utterance and dialogue are not a concern for Marxism and Formalism, utterance and dialogue are the centers of value for the truth Bakhtin has to offer.* Bakhtin's thought does not address the task of the critical reader as a choice between energies released by theme, as against energies released by the literary medium— whether that be prose or poetry. His most capacious commentators know this; for example, Peter Hitchcock at a 2001 conference spoke of what Marx might teach Bakhtin, but also of what Bakhtin needed to teach Marx and Marxians; Hitchcock's prescription: "reading Bakhtin against his own compulsions," which is in fact something I have done in the present book. In today's scholarship, there are few Anglo-American or Russian Formalists out there, doing studies of texts according to Bakhtin's vocabulary. To name some names, I do not regard Gary Saul Morson, Caryl Emerson, Michael Holquist, Vitaly Makhlin, and Mikhail Ryklin as Formalists, though they are certainly not liberationists. There are, however, many capable and lively scholars on the left working with and on Bakhtin; for instance, Peter Hitchcock, David Shepherd, Ken Hirschkop, Craig Brandist, and E. San Juan, Jr. are admirably eager to document Bakhtin's resistance to their views on society and history. They have no wish to change or reject Bakhtin. Where they disagree with him, they say so. Increasingly, scholarship in the spirit of Bakhtin will not be an application of the vocabularies of dialogism and utterance to wider ranges of different texts, but rather a statement of how far an account coincides with Bakhtin's vocabulary and thought, and where the point of divergence should be marked. With Bakhtin's thought, we need to be explicit about where traveling *with* turns into traveling *beyond*.

Marxist or not? Author of certain twenties works, or not? Builder of systematic philosophy, or not? From what we know and are likely to find out, these questions are not cleanly, definitely decidable. In this book I have elected to keep these questions open, and to remain, usually, somewhat behind any points of divergence from Bakhtin's positions on society and communication. Where I have exceeded him in chapter 4, it has been on a question of rhythmic medium and not of theme.

To take *social*, the adjective in this book's title, in a huge and direct sense, as precondition of language and communication and meaning, is consonant with Bakhtin's idea of discourse as the subject of discourse. To take *social* in an exponential sense, as commitment to social positions with poetry, within poetry, upon poetry of the present and past, within commentary on poetry, is entirely appropriate—so long as one marks off the degree to which one's reading has a footing in Bakhtin's own accounts of language and culture. In a book where I have attempted to build a base for a poetics of utterance, I have taken the idea of the social in the direct sense.

The last thing I know about Bakhtin is that, but not exactly where, Bakhtin stops. This proponent of the creative and the unfinalized does stop, because he knows that dialogue requires a silence that is not a termination.

It is entirely possible to respect, and then exceed the framework of thought that an original teacher has built; but in this quite special case I have a warning for those who would follow my own selective representation of Mikhail Bakhtin. Drafting this afterword last, when I imagined I had surpassed Bakhtin's understanding of literary discourse and social struggle, I began to meet him—as he was returning from the beyond, formulating ideas I did not think he could reach. Not for nothing is he famous as the Master of (his term) Unfinalizability. It can only encourage and cheer us that work in his spirit is without end. This is so because as a Master of Dialogue he stops to let us reply. We might keep reading in, with, and beyond Bakhtin—then if needed, beyond the beyond, back to Bakhtin.

Notes

CHAPTER 1. THE SOCIAL MOORINGS OF POETRY

1. Mikhail Bakhtin, from "Methodology for the Human Sciences," in *Speech Genres and Other Late Essays*, trans. Vern W. McGee, ed. Caryl Emerson and Michael Holquist (Austin: University of Texas Press, 1986), 169.

2. Ken Hirschkop, *Mikhail Bakhtin: An Aesthetic for Democracy* (Oxford: Oxford University Press, 1999). This is the most comprehensive and scholarly reading of Bakhtin from a left perspective. Hirschkop is highly persuasive when he shows that there are elements in Bakhtin's makeup that resist a reading of Bakhtin from a left perspective, and thus when he writes against his own hopes and the drift of his argument.

3. Bakhtin's exposition of the "non-alibi in Being" occurs in *Toward a Philosophy of the Act*, trans. with notes by Vadim Liapunov, ed. Vadim Liapunov and Michael Holquist (Austin: University of Texas Press, 1993), pp. 40–46.

4. See Steven Cassedy, *Flight From Eden: The Origins of Modern Literary Criticism and Theory* (Berkeley: University of California Press, 1990).

5. This has already been exhaustively argued by Don H. Bialostosky in a ground breaking book on utterance on *Wordsworth, Dialogics, and the Practice of Criticism* (Cambridge: Cambridge University Press, 1992). I reviewed this book in *Studies in Romanticism* 32, no. 2 (Summer 1993): 311–17. Also fundamental for the dialogic approach generally is Bialostosky's "Dialogics as an Art of Discourse in Literary Criticism," *PMLA* 101, no. 5 (October 1986): 788–97.

The process of working with Bakhtin on poetry is already well advanced in admirable studies by these writers: Will Batstone, "Catullus and Bakhtin: The Problems of a Dialogic Lyric," in *Bakhtin and the Classics*, ed. R. Bracht Branham (Evanston, Ill: Northwestern University Press, 2001); 99–136; Catherine Ciepiela, "Taking Monologism Seriously: Bakhtin and Tsvetaeva's 'The Pied Piper,'" *Slavic Review* 53, no. 4 (Winter 1994): 1010–24; Caryl Emerson, "Poetics with a Loophole: Bakhtin and the Russian Formalist Tradition," paper presented at the MLA Panel Presentation of the early 1990s; Emerson, "Prosaics and the Problem of Form," *Slavic and East European Journal* 41, no. 1 (1997): 16–39; David H. Richter, "Dialogism and Poetry," *Studies in the Literary Imagination* (Spring 1990): 9–27; Lynn J. Shakhinovsky, "Hidden Listeners: Dialogism in the Poetry of Emily Dickinson," *Discours Social/Social Discourse* 3, nos. 1–2 (Spring–Summer 1990): 199–215; Mara Scanlon, "Heteroglossia in Derek Walcott's *Omeros*," *Bakhtin and the Nation*, a special issue of *The Bucknell Review*, ed. San Diego Bakhtin Circle (Lewisburg, Penn: Bucknell University Press): 101–17. These are the articles I have found most brilliant, both for the Bakhtin they convey and for their readings of poems. Using the combined rubrics of Bakhtin and poetry, a journal search of the last twenty years of publications will yield over 130 titles.

6. Mikhail Bakhtin, from "Discourse in the Novel" in *The Dialogic Imagination: Four Essays*, trans. Caryl Emerson and Michael Holquist, ed. Michael Holquist (Austin: University of Texas Press, 1981), 360.

7. V. N. Voloshinov, "Discourse in Life and Discourse in Poetry," trans. John Richmond, in *Bakhtin School Papers*, ed. Ann Shukman (Oxford: Russian Poetics in Translation, 1983), 5–30.

8. In utterance-study prior to the present book, these are among the notable landmarks: Bialostosky, *Wordsworth and Criticism*, on speakers and speech-acts in Wordsworth; Robert Crawford, *Identifying Poets* (Edinburgh: Edinburgh University Press, 1993), a study on heteroglossia and dialect in world literature in English, with a special emphasis on the three languages of Scotland; a theoretical essay by Caryl Emerson, "The Outer Word and Inner Speech: Bakhtin, Vygotsky, and the Internalization of Language," in *Bakhtin: Essays and Dialogues on His Work*, ed. Gary Saul Morson, (Chicago: University of Chicago Press, 1986); Nicholas Zavialoff, "L'Enunciation chez Bakhtine: Une explication restrictive," in *L'Heritage de Mikhail Bakhtine*, ed. Catherine Depretto (Bordeaux: Presses Universitaires de Bordeaux, 1997).

In intonation study, a subset of utterance, Stefania Sini has a capacious and careful synthesis of all Bakhtin's references to social tones in rhetoric: "Intonation, Tone, and Accent in Mikhail Bakhtin's Thought," in the Mikhail Bakhtin and the Future of Signs issue of *Recherches Sémiotique/Semiotic Inquiry* 18, nos. 1–2 (1998): 39–58.

9. Dana Polan, "A Typology of the Intellectual Cultural Critic," in *Discontinuous Discourses in Modern Russian Literature*, ed. Catriona Kelly, Michael Makin, and David Shepherd (Houndmills: Macmillan, 1989), 9. Polan's insight here seems to resonate with, and perhaps even to derive from, an insight of Ken Hirschkop's published three years earlier. The implications of Hirschkop's idea have yet to be worked out for our understanding of the social moorings of literature. He wrote in 1986: "meaning lies neither in text nor context but in the relation between them . . . dialogism and monologism are not different kinds of texts, but different kinds of intertextual configuration" ("The Domestication of M. M. Bakhtin," *Essays in Poetics* 11, no. 1 [1986], 81).

10. There is a capacious framing of discourse in politics in Roland Barthes's essays on languages of social subversion from the 1950s and 1960s, many of the best collected in *The Rustle of Language*, trans. Richard Howard (New York: Hill and Wang, 1986). Barthes did not then know about Bakhtin, but he anticipated ways of giving a sharper edge to Bakhtin's account of public language.

More explicitly in the line of Bakhtin, I would here praise work on ideologemes or coded social themes in Yuri Streidter, Graham Pechey, and Dana Polan; and in Robert Crawford's editorial statement, "Bakhtin and Scotlands," in the first issue of *Scotlands* (Edinburgh: Edinburgh University Press, 1996).

11. "The Dialectical Criticism of Poetry: An Instance from Keats," in The Sociological Perspectives on Literature issue of *Mosaic* 5, no. 2 (Winter 1972): 81–96.

12. David Shepherd, "Bakhtin and the Reader," in *Bakhtin and Cultural Theory*, ed. Ken Hirschkop and David Shepherd, 2d ed. (Manchester: Manchester University Press, 2001), 151.

13. Galin Tihanov, *The Master and the Slave: Lukács, Bakhtin, and the Ideas of Their Time* (Oxford University Press, 2000).

14. See notes 6 and 12 for references to these two books, and please note that only the 1989 first edition of *Bakhtin and Cultural Theory* contains a glossary. An

advance sampling of a larger such project, underway by Gary Saul Morson and Caryl Emerson, is their "Extracts from a *Heteroglossary*," in *Dialogue and Critical Discourse: Language, Culture, Critical Theory*, ed. Michael Macovski (Oxford: Oxford University Press, 1997).

15. The summary in the next three paragraphs will rely on notes I took, at a 1982 lecture by Michael Holquist (Humanities Conference, Stanford University). Holquist never published this succinct summary, so in this odd Bakhtinian convergence, Holquist's words and mine are inextricable; while I cannot place quotation marks here, he definitely owns the larger share of the double-voicing.

16. The constitutive work is Lev Vygotsky, *Thought and Language*, ed. and trans. Eugenia Hanfman and Gertrude Vakar (Cambridge: MIT Press, 1962). The first Russian edition was 1934. There is no proof Bakhtin read Vygotsky; on the convergence of their ideas of communication, see James V. Wertsch, *Voices of the Mind: A Sociocultural Approach to Mediated Action* (Cambridge: Harvard University Press, 1991). A thoughtful survey of Russian work on the topic, before and after Vygotsky, is A. N. Sokolov, *Inner Speech and Thought*, trans. George T. Onischenko (New York: Plenum Press, 1972).

17. The two quoted passages under the heading of POETRY come from "Discourse in the Novel," 285, and from "Supplement: The Problem of Content, Materials, and Form in Verbal Art" (1924), trans. Kenneth Brostrom, in *Art and Answerability: Early Philosophical Essays*, ed. Michael Holquist and Vadim Liapunov, trans. with notes by Vadim Liapunov (Austin: University of Texas Press, 1990), 294.

18. Michael Holquist, *Dialogism: Bakhtin and His World* (London: Routledge, 1990), 20–21.

19. This is Michael Holquist's Glossary definition in *The Dialogic Imagination*, 425.

20. Ibid., 425.

21. Ibid., 429.

22. Ibid., 434.

23. "Autonomous voice" is Holquist's phrase, *The Dialogic Imagination*, 432. Michael Davidson's "propositions of 'subject'" is from his splendid brief study, "Discourse in Poetry: Bakhtin and Extensions of the Dialogical," in *Code of Signals: Recent Writings in Poetics*, ed. Michael Palmer (Berkeley: North Atlantic Books, 1983), from which I quote a sentence that could set the agenda for work with and beyond Bakhtin: "What is needed is a critique of poetry not based upon the authorial expressive subject but rather upon the propositions of 'subject' generated by specific ideological discourses" (149). See also below my section on the speaking subject.

24. Caryl Emerson, preface to *Problems of Dostoevsky's Poetics*, by Mikhail Bakhtin, ed. and trans. Caryl Emerson (Minneapolis: University of Minnesota Press, 1984), xxxiv, xxxii.

25. Caryl Emerson, "Bakhtin, Lotman, Vygotski, and Lydia Ginsburg on Types of Selves: A Tribute," in *Self and Story in Russian History*, ed. Laura Engelstein and Stephanie Sandler (Ithaca: Cornell University Press, 2000), 31.

26. Wlad Godzich, "Bakhtin and Intercultural Interactions," *boundary* 2 (Spring 1991), 16, 17.

27. With minor changes, this and the next three paragraphs come from my article, "The Speaking Subject in Russian Poetry and Poetics Since 1917," *New Literary History* 23 (1992), 93, 103–5. Reprinted by permission of Ralph Cohen, editor of *New Literary History*.

28. Marina Tsvetaeva, *Poet* (The Poet), in *Sochineniia v dvukh tomakh*, vol. 1 (Moscow, Khudozhestvennaya Literatura 1984), 235 (my translation).

29. Bulat Okudzhava, *65 Songs/65 Pesen*, ed. Vladimir Frumkin, 4th ed. (Ann Arbor: Ardis, 1988), 88–89; Vassily Aksyonov, review of *65 Songs/65 Pesen*, by Bulat Okudzhava, in *Times Literary Supplement*, 28 March 1986, 38.

30. See Gerald Stanton Smith, *Songs to Seven Strings: Russian Guitar Poetry and Soviet 'Mass Song'* (Bloomington: Indiana University Press, 1984).

31. This is the focus of the book I wrote with Tadeusz Slawek, *Literary Voice: The Calling of Jonah* (Albany: State University of New York Press, 1995).

32. "Discourse in the Novel," 337.

33. See Sokolov, *Inner Speech*; and Caryl Emerson's pathbreaking article, which has influenced all who think about this topic in the English-speaking world: "The Outer Word and Inner Speech: Bakhtin, Vygotsky, and the Internalization of Language," in *Bakhtin: Essays and Dialogues on his Work*, ed. Gary Saul Morson (Chicago: University of Chicago Press, 1986).

34. Holquist, *Dialogism*, 51.

35. The translation used is John Richmond's in *Bakhtin School Papers*, 111; hereafter in my text, page references are to this translation.

36. P. N. Medvedev, *The Formal Method in Literary Scholarship*, trans. Albert J. Wehrle (Cambridge: Harvard University Press, 1985), 126, 133–34.

37. Caryl Emerson, "The Outer Word and Inner Speech," 35.

38. Mikhail Bakhtin, *Problems of Dostoevsky's Poetics*, ed. and trans. Caryl Emerson (Minneapolis: University of Minnesota Press, 1984), 256, 235.

39. Holquist, "Discourse in the Novel," 319. My quotations touch only the most relevant points of a passage several pages long, all of which deserves close attention.

40. "The Problem of the Text," *Speech Genres and Other Late Essays*, ed. Caryl Emerson and Michael Holquist, trans. Vern W. McGee (Austin: University of Texas Press, 1986), 106, 119.

41. Dwight Bollinger, *Intonation and Its Parts* (Stanford: Stanford University Press, 1986), x, 3.

42. In this paragraph, references to Voloshinov quote or paraphrase from his "Discourse in Life and Discourse in Poetry," in *Bakhtin School Papers*, 25, 15. Caryl Emerson's phrase, on tone as "the proper clamp between culture and life," occurs in her review article, "Bakhtin at 100: Looking Back at the Very Early Years," *The Russian Review* 54 (January 1995), 110.

43. Juliet Flower MacCannell, "The Temporality of Textuality: Bachtin [*sic*] and Derrida," *MLN* 100, no. 5 (December 1985), Stefania Sini's important essay is "Intonation, Tone, and Accent in Mikhail Bakhtin's Thought," in the Mikhail Bakhtin and the Future of Signs issue of *Recherches Sémiotiques/Semiotic Inquiry* 18, nos. 1–2 (Montréal: Canadian Semiotic Association, 1998): 39–58.

44. The social moorings of poetry are stronger and more obvious in the genre of satire, by comparison with lyric. Two essays on Pope show this especially well: Ronald Schleifer, "Enunciation and Genre: Mikhail Bakhtin and the 'Double-Voiced Narration' of 'The Rape of the Lock,'" *New Orleans Review* 15, no. 4 (Winter 1988): 31–42; Mary Ellen Bellanca, "Alien Voices, Ancient Echoes: Bakhtin, Dialogism, and Pope's Essay on Criticism," *Papers on Language and Literature* 30, no. 1 (Winter 1994): 57–72.

45. "Discourse in the Novel," 335, 336. The emphasis is Bakhtin's. References to this essay in the next few paragraphs will be incorporated in my text.

46. Several readers of Chaucer who have found Bakhtin useful are Jaewhan Kim, "The Genre of the Canterbury Tales," *The Journal of English Language and Literature* (Seoul, Korea) 38, no. 2 (Summer 1992): 213–27; James Andreas, " 'Newe Science' from 'Olde Bokes': A Bakhtinian Approach to the Summoner's Tale," in *Chaucer Review* 23 (1990): 138–151; Lars Engle, "Chaucer, Bakhtin, and Griselda," in *Exemplaria: A Journal of Theory in Medieval and Renaissance Studies* 1, 2 (1989): 429–59.

CHAPTER 2. BAKHTIN AND THE SOCIAL POETICS OF DIALECT

1. "Unrelated Incidents (3)" is reprinted by permission of Tom Leonard; "It dread inna Inglan" is reprinted by permission of Linton Kwesi Johnson who holds the copyright. The author and editors gratefully acknowledge the cooperation and support of Tom Leonard, Linton Kwesi Johnson, and their respective publishers.

2. Tom Leonard, *Intimate Voices: Selected Work 1965–1983* (Newcastle-Upon-Tyne: Galloping Dog, 1983).

3. Linton Kwesi Johnson, "It dread inna Inglan," *Inglan is a bitch* (London: Race Today, 1980).

4. P. N. Medvedev and M. M. Bakhtin, *The Formal Method in Literary Scholarship: A Critical Introduction to Sociological Poetics*, trans. Albert J. Wehrle (Baltimore: Johns Hopkins University Press, 1978), 80–81.

5. Mikhail Bakhtin, "Discourse in the Novel," *The Dialogic Imagination: Four Essays*, trans. Caryl Emerson and Michael Holquist, ed. Michael Holquist (Austin: University of Texas Press, 1981), 294.

6. Mikhail Bakhtin, *Rabelais and His World*, trans. Hélène Iswolsky (Bloomington: Indiana University Press, 1984), 468.

7. Roland Barthes, "The Division of Languages," *The Rustle of Language*, trans. Richard Howard (New York: Hill and Wang, 1986), 111–24.

8. Gilles Deleuze and Félix Guattari, *Kafka: Toward a Minor Literature*, trans. Dana Polan (Minneapolis: University of Minnesota Press, 1986), 16.

9. Bakhtin's most developed account of temporal rhythm in fiction occurs in the early study "Author and Hero in Aesthetic Activity" (c. 1920–23), *Art and Answerability: Early Philosophical Essays*, trans. with notes by Vadim Liapunov, ed. Michael Holquist and Vadim Liapunov, trans. and notes Vadim Liapunov (Austin: University of Texas Press, 1990), esp. 112–21 and 219–17. The whole issue of Bakhtin's view of rhythm as it changed over time, and as he uses the term to justify a preference for fiction, has not been studied to the bottom. I will have more to say on this question in chapter 4.

10. For Bakhtin the artistic representation of a language, "discourse as the subject of discourse" ("Discourse" 337), is the central problem for a social stylistics of the novel. For me, it is the central problem for a social stylistics of dialect poetry.

11. Bryan Appleyard, *The Pleasures of Peace: Art and Imagination in Post-War Britain* (Boston: Faber, 1989).

12. Hugh Seton-Watson, *Nations and States: An Enquiry into the Origins of Nations and the Politics of Nationalism* (London: Methuen, 1977), 42.

13. Ralf Dahrendorf, *On Britain* (Chicago: University of Chicago Press, 1982), 51.

14. Ibid., 156.

15. Fred D'Aguilar, introduction to *The New British Poetry*, ed. Gillian Allnett et al. (London: Paladin-Grafton, 1988), 3.

16. E. J. Hobsbawm, *Nations and Nationalism Since 1780: Programme, Myth, Reality* (Cambridge: Cambridge University Press, 1990), 181.

17. Arthur Hughes and Peter Trudgill, *English Accents and Dialects*, 2d ed. (London: E. Arnold, 1979); Valerie Shepherd, *Language Variety and the Art of the Everyday* (New York: Pinter, 1990).

18. Tony Crowley, *The Politics of Discourse: The Standard Language Question in British Cultural Debates* (Houndmills, Eng.: Macmillan Education, 1989).

19. The distinction between border and diaspora cultures is one I have learned from James Clifford's lecture on "Dwelling/Traveling: Late 20th Century Intercultures," San Diego Museum of Contemporary Art, 9 April 1991, a part of which was published as "The Transit Lounge of Culture" *Times Literary Supplement*, 3 May 1991, 7–8.

20. Reading David Craig's *On the Crofter's Trail* (London: Cape, 1990), after this essay had been drafted, reminded me that Scotland has been a diaspora culture as well as a border culture: the Clearances of the early nineteenth century sent the Highlanders and Islanders all over the world, primarily to Nova Scotia and eastern Canada.

21. Tom Nairn argues the Scottish Enlightenment in eighteenth century Edinburgh was in rapport with modes of production and types of culture widely various, yet co-existing in Lowlands rational agriculture, Highlands archaic clans in a subsistence and quasifeudal economy, Islands with their weaving and fishing and a small, nearly unreachable population. For Nairn, this was the precondition for Scotland's failure to theorize itself as a nation, and to split from England: *The Break-Up of Britain: Crisis and Neo-Nationalism* (London: NLB, 1977). See also T. C. Smout, *A History of the Scottish People, 1560–1830* (London: Collins, 1969).

22. Leonard, "Parokial," in *Intimate Voices*, 4–11.

23. For Leonard on William Carlos Williams, see the essay "The Locust Tree in Flower, and Why It Has Difficulty Flowering in Britain," *Intimate Voices*, 95–102.

24. In a three-volume work published in 1971 but announced in less guarded articles in the 1960s, Basil Bernstein developed his influential distinction between the elaborated cultural and linguistic codes of the middle class and the restricted codes of the working class. See esp. volume 1 of *Class Codes and Control: Theoretical Studies Towards a Sociology of Language* (London: Routledge and Kegan Paul, 1971). One negative judgment is Harold Rosen's pamphlet, *Language and Class: A Critical Look at the Theories of Basil Bernstein* (Bristol: Falling Wall, 1972, 1974).

25. C. L. R. James, *Beyond a Boundary* (London: Hutchinson, 1963).

26. Louise Bennett, *Jamaica Labrish* (Kingston, Jamaica: Songster's Book Stores, 1966).

27. Sheila Rule, "Black Britons Describe a Motherland That Has Long Held Them as Inferior," *New York Times*, 31 March 1991, A6.

28. Paul Gilroy, *There Ain't No Black in the Union Jack* (London: Hutchinson, 1987), 219. Peter Fryer, *Staying Power: The History of Black People in Britain* (London: Pluto, 1984); Paul B. Rich, *Race and Empire in British Politics*, 2d ed. (Cambridge: Cambridge University Press, 1990).

29. Both for its use of Deleuze-Guattari on minor literature, and for its range of examples, I have found the best study to be Patrick Williams's "Difficult Subjects: Black British Women's Poetry," chapter 6 of *Literary Theory and Poetry*, ed. D. J. Murray (London: Batsford, 1989).

30. F. G. Roelehr, "A Look at New Expressions in the Arts of the Contemporary Caribbean," *Caribbean Quarterly* 17 nos. 3–4 (1971), 108.

31. Cornel West, "Black Culture and Postmodernism," *Remaking History*, ed. Barbara Kruger and Phil Mariani (Seattle: Bay, 1989).

91. The phrase comes from "Discourse in the Novel," where Bakhtin of course makes no reference to English (357).

Chapter 3. "Easier to Die than to Remember"

1. Reading the poem while following an audiotape of the performing author is the reader-response complement to the method Bunting proposed for writers: "Compose aloud: poetry is a sound" ("I SUGGEST," Bunting's advice to student poets in Newcastle, published by the Basil Bunting Poetry Archive, Durham University, in the form of a postcard available from Palace Green Library, Durham DH1 3RN). Throughout my text, the abbreviation *CP* refers to page numbers in *Collected Poems: Basil Bunting* (Tarset, Northumberland: Bloodaxe Books, 2000); *UP* refers to *Basil Bunting: Uncollected Poems*, ed. Richard Caddel (Oxford: Oxford University Press, 1991).

2. Mikhail Bakhtin, *Speech Genres and Other Late Essays*, trans. Vern W. McGee, ed. Caryl Emerson and Michael Holquist (Austin: University of Texas Press, 1986), 147.

3. Victoria Forde, *The Poetry of Basil Bunting* (Newcastle: Bloodaxe Books, 1991), 12; my emphasis.

4. Peter Makin, *Bunting: The Shaping of His Verse* (Oxford: Oxford University Press, 1992).

5. Mikhail Bakhtin, *The Dialogic Imagination: Four Essays*, trans. Caryl Emerson and Michael Holquist, ed. Michael Holquist (Austin: University of Texas Press, 1981), 293.

6. Bakhtin, *Speech Genres*, 169.

7. The four previous sentences are from my notes on a lecture about Bakhtin given by Michael Holquist at the Humanities Institute, Stanford University, Stanford, CA, Summer 1982.

8. Bunting's "Such syllables flicker out of grass" is Ode 11 in *UP*, 22. Victoria Forde's admirable biographical treatment of the poem is essential to any interpretation: *Poetry of Basil Bunting*, 242–47.

9. From the Soviet twenties onward, when Lev Vygotsky founded a psycholinguistic school and Bakhtin founded a philosophical one, Russian thinkers have had a social understanding of inner speech. Vygotsky's thought is concerned with human development. Bakhtin and his circle, by contrast, study fully mature inner speech, interested in development only in the sense that the person is never fully fixed, always learning through the need to negotiate across the boundary between inner consciousness and the outside world. And language, as Caryl Emerson notes, is the "energy negotiating between," so language is not, for Bakhtin, a "product or detachable attribute of a person" (translator's introduction to Mikhail Bakhtin, *Problems of Dostoevsky's Poetics* [Minneapolis: University of Minneapolis Press, 1984], p.xxxiv). Voloshinov's book *Freudianism: A Critical Sketch* (1927) (Bloomington: Indiana University Press, 1987) is by far the weakest of the Bakhtin Circle's efforts, since it attacks psychoanalysis as a bourgeois science on the basis of limited knowl-

edge of Freud's works, but the book is useful in its clear, perhaps overclear, distinction between inner speech and the unconscious. Voloshinov sets inner speech, a linguistic gauge of cultural development, against the unconscious, which cannot exist, except as a deluxe myth, because it operates before or without language. Neal H. Bruss in a recent appendix to the Indiana edition of this book argues that nascent Freudianism and nascent Structuralism might have converged more successfully in the twenties had both sides in this debate known what they shared in the "emphasis on the linguistic foundation of personhood" (*Freudianism* 139). What I admire in Voloshinov's book and in his two articles on discourse in *Bakhtin School Papers*, ed. Ann Shukman (Oxford: Russian Poetics in Translation 10, 1983), is his stress on conflicts between inner speech and outer speech and between different levels of inner speech, and his statement, that "The style of a poet is engendered from the style of his inner speech . . . , and his inner speech is itself the product of his entire social life" (quoting here from the translation of "Discourse in Life and Discourse in Poetry," in Bakhtin School Papers, 27; translation modified).

Pavel Medvedev's book about *The Formal Method in Literary Scholarship* (1928), trans. Albert J. Wehrle (Baltimore: Johns Hopkins University Press, 1978), has similar sociological aims, this time directed to home-grown Russian literary scholarship that speaks of defamiliarizing the device, and that puts stylistics and literary history into the psychology of the reader and takes reified particles as things to study. Against this, dialogism would say "Only the utterance can be beautiful [and] true." My essay pursues the implications of this for critical reading.

10. Lev Vygotsky in his profound and profoundly Marxist book, *Thought and Language* (1934), argued that thought and speech have different genetic roots, and these two functions meet and intertwine at about the early school years when the child is taught language, logic, and cultural norms: *Thought and Language*, ed. and trans. Eugenia Hanfmann and Gertrude Vakar (Cambridge: MIT Press, 1962). Vygotsky proposed a three-stage model: external speech when the child drinks in from parents and culture; egocentric speech when the child begins to appreciate the social aspects of language, and puts itself at the center of the universe; and inner speech, the highest and most mature, when the child can turn "the predicative, idiomatic structure of inner speech into syntactically articulated speech intelligible to others" (148). James V. Wertsch compares Vygotsky and Bakhtin at length on inner and outer speech in *Voices of the Mind: A Sociocultural Approach to Mediated Action* (Cambridge: Harvard University Press, 1991).

Vygotsky said inner speech is composed *mostly of verbs* (145). One scholar working in the line of Vygotsky, N. I. Zhinkin, whose writings were known to Bakhtin, held that inner speech lacks the redundancy of external language, and is more like "an objective pictorial code." (Zhinkin is here summarized and quoted by A. A. Leont'ev in one of the contributions to James V. Wertsch, ed., *Recent Trends in Soviet Psycholinguistics* [White Plains, N.Y.: M. E. Sharpe, 1977], 14–15.) Certainly inner speech is speech minus sound, but it also has a distinct positive function. For Bakhtin it was a "variegated verbal dance" with images, schemata, symbols, and phonetic fragments, all more or less verbal or capable of being verbalized. In the most explicit statement of the nature of units, Voloshinov in *Marxism and the Philosophy of Language* (1929) said that "the units of which inner speech is constituted are certain whole entities . . . most of all they resemble *alternating lines of dialogue*. There was good reason why thinkers in ancient times would have conceived of inner speech as *inner dialogue*" (trans. Ladislav Matejka and I. R. Titunik [New York: Seminar, 1973], 38).

11. See especially Gary Saul Morson and Caryl Emerson, *Mikhail Bakhtin: Creation of a Prosaics* (Stanford: Stanford University Press, 1990), 200–28.

12. Caryl Emerson, "The Outer Word and Inner Speech," in *Bakhtin: Essays and Dialogues on his Work*, ed. Gary Saul Morson (Chicago: University of Chicago Press, 1986), 35.

13. George Steiner, "The Distribution of Discourse," in *One Difficulty and Other Essays* (Oxford: Oxford University Press, 1978), 94.

14. Medvedev and Bakhtin, *The Formal Method in Literary Scholarship*, 84, 126.

15. Michael Holquist, *Dialogism: Bakhtin and His World* (London: Routledge, 1990), 51.

16. Peter Dale, "Basil Bunting and the Quonk and Groggle School of Poetry," *Agenda* 16: no. 1 (Spring 1978): 55–65.

17. Bakhtin, *Speech Genres*, 89.

18. The version of "Per che no spero" with the final clause appears in *Agenda* 16, no. 1 (1978), 5, with the date 1977 below the poem.

19. Warren Tallman and Peter Quartermain, "Basil Bunting Talks about *Briggflatts*," *Georgia Straight Writing Supplement* 6 (1970): n.p.

20. James Moffett, "Writing, Inner Speech, and Meditation," typescript of an essay from the late 1970s (personal copy).

21. One more of the handful of "I SUGGEST" imperatives in Bunting's Newcastle statement, note 1 above.

22. My thanks to Robert Creeley for showing to me a photocopy of the Sonnets with these amazing deletions.

23. Quoted in Makin, *Shaping*, 156.

24. Peter Quartermain, *Basil Bunting: Poet of the North*, printed as a pamphlet by the Basil Bunting Poetry Archive (Durham, 1990).

25. Of the several in the Don Juan series by Carlos Castaneda, the one with the most on internal dialogue is *Separate Reality: Further Conversations with Don Juan* (New York: Pocket Books, 1972).

26. Lisa Kenner, Hugh Kenner's daughter, described this in the Bunting tribute issue of *Conjunctions* 8 (1985).

27. Bakhtin, *Speech Genres*, 133–34; my emphasis.

28. (New York: Plenum Press, 1972).

Chapter 4. Rhythmic Cognition in the Reader

1. Gary Saul Morson and Caryl Emerson, *Mikhail Bakhtin: Creation of a Prosaics* (Stanford: Stanford University Press, 1990), 20 (for all passages quoted.)

2. Mikhail Bakhtin, *Towards a Philosophy of the Act*, trans. Vadim Liapunov (Austin: University of Texas Press, 1994); Mikhail Bakhtin, "Author and Hero in Aesthetic Activity," *Art and Answerability: Early Philosophical Essays by M. M. Bakhtin*, trans. with notes by Vadim Liapunov, ed. Michael Holquist and Vadim Liapunov (Austin: University of Texas Press, 1990). Hereafter, these essays will be cited in the text as *TPA* and *AH*, respectively.

3. See Don H. Bialostosky, *Wordsworth, Dialogics and the Practice of Criticism* (Cambridge: Cambridge University Press, 1992); Robert Crawford, *Identifying Poets: Self and Territory in Twentieth-Century Poetry* (Edinburgh: Edinburgh University Press, 1993); and Lynn J. Shakinovsky, "Hidden Listeners: Dialogism in the Poetry of

Emily Dickinson," *Social Discourse/Discours Social* 3, nos. 1–2 (Spring–Summer 1990): 199–214.

4. Lily Feiler, *Marina Tsvetaeva: The Double Beat of Heaven and Hell* (Durham: Duke University Press, 1994), esp. 140–41 for sentences on "Wires" and Feiler's quotation of Tsvetaeva's tribute to Pasternak, "brother in the fifth season and in the fourth dimension"; Catherine Ciepiela, "The Demanding Woman Poet: On Resisting Marina Tsvetaeva," *PMLA* 111, no. 3 (May 1996): 421–34 (quote on 428). It will not be part of my assignment to show, against Bakhtin and Ciepiela, that poetry can be "dialogical"; see Ciepiela's important article "Taking Monologism Seriously: Bakhtin and Tsvetaeva's 'The Pied Piper'," *Slavic Review* 53 no. 4 (Winter 1994): 1010–24, in which she proposes that if we accept Bakhtin's sense, one would first have to demonstrate the presence of ideological languages and then analyze the manner of their orchestration: "are they monologically suppressed or dialogically allowed to speak their plural truths?" (1014). Absolutely the right question.

5. Mikhail Bakhtin, "Discourse in the Novel," in *The Dialogic Imagination: Four Essays*, trans. Caryl Emerson and Michael Holquist, ed. Michael Holquist (Austin: University of Texas Press, 1981), 298; Bakhtin's emphasis.

6. The Russian text of the first poem in the series "Provoda" is taken, under fair use based on international publishing agreements at the time of original publication, from Marina Tsvetaeva, *Izbrannye Proizvedeniia* (Moscow-Leningrad: Sovetskii Pisatel'/Biblioteka Poeta, 1965), vol. 1, 225–26. The English translation is reprinted with permission of the translator who owns the rights from Marina Tsvetaeva, *After Russia/Posle Rosii*, trans. Michael M. Naydan with Slava Yastremski, annotated by Michael M. Naydan (Ann Arbor: Ardis, 1992), 97–99. Elaine Feinstein's English free-verse translation, which preserves the line of images but sacrifices meter, rhyme, stanza structure, and punctuation, is not only a failure (all translations are failures), but a travesty. Eve Malleret's French versions of Tsvetaeva's even greater long poems of the same era, "Poem of the Mountain" and "Poem of the End," are far more satisfactory with similar short-line stanza poems of lost love. Malleret finds French substitutes for the original rhyme, meter and punctuation: Marina Tsvetaeva, *Le Poème de la montagne/Le Poème de la fin*, trans. and introduced Eve Malleret (Lausanne: Éditions L'Age d'Homme, 1984). Malleret's Tsvetaeva is Meschonnic's topic for the title essay of his *La Rime et la vie* (Paris: Éditions Verdier, 1989), in which he argues that Malleret uniquely catches the violence of sound in Tsvetaeva, a violence that is an "oralization of language"; consequently, "to freeverse [Tsvetaeva] is to break her principle of organization, her language, her rapport with the 19th century" (227, 219, my translation).

7. Yuri Tynianov, *The Problem of Verse Language*, trans. M. Sousa and Brent Harvey (Ann Arbor: Ardis, 1981), esp. 62.

8. Émile Benveniste, "La notion du 'rythme' dans son expression linguistique" (1951), in *Problèmes de linguistique générale* (Paris: Gallimard, 1966), 327–35; I quote here from Meschonnic's summary and comment in *Critique du rythme: anthropologie historique du langage* (Paris: Edition Verdier, 1982), 69–73.

9. Richard Cureton, *Rhythmic Phrasing in Enlish Verse* (London: Longman, 1992); I am more convinced by Richard Cureton's demonstration that weak-strong contrasts operate at the lowest and mid-levels of phrasing than I am by his contrasts at the highest levels, i.e., above sentence and line. In my own related book I argue that the most volatile and significant energy of thought is produced by the relationship of sentence and line, when these are coincident or noncoincident: *The Scissors of Meter: Grammetrics and Reading* (Ann Arbor: University of Michigan Press, 1996).

10. Simon Karlinsky, *Marina Cvetaeva: Her Life and Art* (Berkeley: University of California Press, 1966), 162.

11. See the brilliant wordplay on the instrumental plural *"próvodami"* ("In the farewells" [line 21]) and genitive plural *"provodóv"* ("of steel wires" [line 22]). The Russian words sound the same but are distinguished by stress (and the restriction of the former to the plural).

12. James H. Bunn, *Wave Forms: A Natural Syntax for Rhythmic Languages* (Stanford: Stanford University Press, 2002). Waves, heartbeats, and other natural forms are agreeable analogues for works of verbal art, but language is not the world. Henri Meschonnic in *Critique du rythme* (1982) has the refutation of Bunn's thesis, twenty years in advance of Bunn's publication—especially in Meschonnic's chapter on wave-forms in Saint-Jean Perse, where he writes, for example, "The poem of Saint-Jean Perse *does not do what it says*. . . . It falls back into dualism. It separates itself into a signifier and a signified" (379); (my translation).

13. Marina Tsvetaeva, *Poet* (The Poet), in *Sochineniia v dvukh tomakh*, vol. 1 (Moscow, Khudozhestvennaya Literatura, 1980), 235; my translation.

14. With certain small changes, this and the next four sentences are taken, with permission, from my article "The Speaking Subject in Russian Poetry and Poetics Since 1917," *New Literary History* (1992), 93–94; please see Acknowledgments.

15. For Meschonnic, see notes 6 and 8 above.

16. Michael Makin, *Marina Tsvetaeva: Poetics of Appropriation* (Oxford: Oxford University Press, 1993).

17. Graham Pechey, "Philosophy and Theology in 'Aesthetic Activity,'" in *Bakhtin and Religion: A Feeling for Faith*, ed. Susan M. Felch and Paul J. Contino (Evanston, Ill: Northwestern University Press, 2001); first published in *Dialogism* 1 (1998).

18. Graham Pechey, "Intercultural, intercreatural: Bakhtin and the Uniqueness of 'Literary Seeing,'" (paper presented at the Gdansk Conference, Tenth International Bakhtin Conference held at the University of Gdansk, Poland, on July 23–27, 2001). My thanks to Graham Pechey for permission to quote from his manuscript essay.

19. In what follows, I take a few sentences from my review of Meschonnic's *Critique du rythme*, published in the now-defunct journal, *Eidos: The International Prosody Bulletin* 1, no. 2 (July 1984), 11–12. All translations from Meschonnic are my own.

CHAPTER 5. CLASH OF DISCOURSES

1. Bakhtin, "Rhetoric, in the measure of its falsity," in "Appunti degli anni 1940–1960" [Notes from the years 1940–1960], trans. into Italian by Margherita De Michiel and Stefania Sini, in Vol. 15 of *Kamen': Rivista de poesia e filosofia* 15 (Piacenza: Editrice Vicolo del Pavone, Gennaio, 2000), 45. Their translation is based upon the Russian original published in M. M. Bakhtin, *Sobranie sochinenii* [*Collected Works*], ed. S. G. Bocharov et al., vol. 5 (Moscow: 1996). All translations from the Italian into English are by me.

2. Bakhtin, "Language in Artistic Literature," in "Notes from the years 1940–1960," *Kamen'*, 57.

3. The answers we find are likely to be tentative, especially when we must admit from the start that the clashes described here are constructions by the critic. Also, I would like to thank Fred V. Randel for reminding me that if my comparison be-

tween men and women writers in the next section is extended to Byron and Percy Bysshe Shelley, generalizations about the women being more progressive than the men (Wordsworth and Coleridge) do not hold. Recent criticism by Nicholas Roe and Jeffrey Cox has made similar claims for Keats's radical politics. Byron, Shelley, and (arguably) Keats all engage many of the political/social issues that are here treated as distinctive to women poets of the period.

4. Jerome J. McGann, *The Romantic Ideology: A Critical Investigation* (Chicago: University of Chicago Press, 1983).

5. Graham Pechey, "Not the Novel: Bakhtin, Poetry, Truth, God," in *Bakhtin and Cultural Theory*, ed. Ken Hirschkop and David Shepherd, rev. and expanded 2d ed. (Manchester: Manchester University Press, 2001).

6. Also, "parody" is not a term we would apply to Wordsworth.

7. As exception to this claim about New Criticism's attitude toward Romantic poems, see the perceptive and sympathetic treatment of Wordsworth's "Michael" in Cleanth Brooks and Robert Penn Warren, *Understanding Poetry* (New York: Holt, Rinehart and Winston, 1967), and of Coleridge's "Rime of the Ancient Mariner" in Robert Penn Warren's celebrated essay, "A Poem of Pure Imagination. An Experiment in Reading," in *Twentieth Century Interpretations of Rime of the Ancient Mariner*, edited by James D. Boulger (Englewood Cliffs, N.Y.: Prentice Hall, 1969).

8. Two landmark books of consciousness criticism are: Geoffrey H. Hartman, *Wordsworth's Poetry: 1787–1814* (New Haven: Yale University Press, 1964); Harold Bloom, ed., *Romanticism and Consciousness: Essays in Criticism* (New York: Norton, 1970).

9. Impressive examples of New Historicist (and related history conscious and canon expanding) work are: James Chandler, *Wordsworth's Second Nature: A Study of the Poetry and Politics* (Chicago: University of Chicago Press, 1984); Marjorie Levinson, *Wordsworth's Great Period Poems: Four Essays* (Cambridge: Cambridge University Press,1986); Alan Liu, *Wordsworth: The Sense of History* (Stanford: Stanford University Press, 1989); Kenneth R. Johnston et al., eds., *Romantic Revolutions: Criticism and Theory* (Bloomington: Indiana University Press, 1990); Mary A. Favret and Nicola J. Watson, eds. *At the Limits of Romanticism: Essays in Cultural, Feminist, and Materialist Criticism* (Bloomington: Indiana University Press, 1994). A skeptical commentary on Liu may be found in David Perkins, *Is Literary History Possible?* (Baltimore: The Johns Hopkins University Press, 1992). An excellent adjunct to historical and literary studies of the period, with essays by two scholars mentioned in these notes, Jerome McGann and James Chandler, is *An Oxford Companion to the Romantic Age: British Culture 1776–1832*, ed. Iain McCalman (Oxford: Oxford University Press, 1999): The essay on slavery by James Walvin is especially pertinent to my comparison, below, of poems by Opie and Wordsworth. I do not know if Kurt Heinzelman considers himself a New Historicist, but his work on the economics of the imagination in Romanticism is entirely pertinent here.

10. At the University of California, San Diego, in the academic year 2001–2, Romanticism was taught in four upper-division courses: First Generation Romantic Poets (Wordsworth, Coleridge, and Women Poets), Romantic Women Poets, Byron and Byronism, and Keats and His Heirs. In the first of these, enrollment doubled from the usual twenty because of the presence of the word "women" in the course title, and three-quarters of students came from majors other than literature. In the second of these, also with a respectable enrollment, the women poets were taught for the most part without reference to the male writers of the period.

11. Margaret Homans, *Women Writers and Poetic Identity: Dorothy Wordsworth, Emily Bronte, and Emily Dickinson* (Princeton, N.J.: Princeton University Press, 1980).

12. Mary Jacobus, "The Law of/and Gender: Genre Theory and *The Prelude*," *Diacritics* (Winter 1984): 47–57; Mary Jacobus, *Reading Woman: Essays in Feminist Criticism* (New York: Columbia University Press, 1986); Mary Jacobus, *Romanticism, Writing, and Sexual Difference* (Oxford: Oxford University Press, 1989).

13. John Barrell, "The Uses of Dorothy: 'The Language of the Sense' in 'Tintern Abbey'," chapter 5 in *Poetry, Language & Politics* (Manchester: Manchester University Press, 1988).

14. Anne K. Mellor, ed., *Romanticism and Feminism* (Bloomington: Indiana University Press, 1988). Related and later, her study of masculine and feminine Romanticisms: Anne K. Mellor, *Romanticism and Gender* (New York: Routledge, 1993).

15. The anthologies in chronological order: Roger Lonsdale, ed., *Eighteenth-Century Women Poets* [containing some writers who produce work after 1789] (Oxford: Oxford University Press, 1989); Andrew Ashfield, ed., *Romantic Women Poets, 1770–1838* (Manchester: Manchester University Press, 1995); Margaret Randolph Higonnet, ed., *British Women Poets of the 19th Century* (New York: Penguin Books, 1996); Duncan Wu, ed., *Romantic Women Poets: An Anthology* (Oxford: Blackwell, 1997). One example of a recent reprinting: Felicia Hemans, *Records of Women: With Other Poems*, ed. Paula R. Feldman (1828; reprinted University Press of Kentucky, 1999).

16. In *Romanticism and Gender*, Anne K. Mellor speaks of the way women writers domesticate the sublime, by "offering an alternative definition of the sublime as an experience that produces an intensified emotional and moral participation in a human community"; and she argues that women writers condemn the Sublime of Burke and Wordsworth "as a moment of masculine empowerment over female nature" (105).

17. The three studies by Tilottama Rajan, here mentioned, are: *Dark Interpreter: The Discourse of Romanticism* (Ithaca: Cornell University Press, 1980); "Romanticism and the Death of Lyric Consciousness," in *Lyric Poetry: Beyond New Criticism*, ed. Chaviva Hosek and Patricia Parker (Ithaca: Cornell University Press, 1985), phrase here quoted from p. 200, and concluding sentences quoted from pp. 206–7; *The Supplement of Reading: Figures of Understanding in Romantic Theory and Practice* (Ithaca: Cornell University Press, 1990).

18. In 1997 I read a just completed Oxford University doctoral thesis on Robert Burns by Liam McIlvanney, which intelligently employed ideas of heteroglossia and carnival; another heteroglossia study is by Gordon Thomas, "The *Lyrical Ballads* Ode: Dialogized Heteroglossia," in *The Wordsworth Circle* (1989): 102–5. Ashton Nichols's book is *The Revolutionary 'I': Wordsworth and the Politics of Self-Presentation* (New York: St. Martin's Press, 1998), here quoted from p. xiii. Three books on the Wordsworth-Coleridge dialogue, which refer to Bakhtin as the primary theorist of dialogue in our era are: Paul Magnuson, *Coleridge and Wordsworth: A Lyrical Dialogue* (Princeton: Princeton University Press, 1988); Gene W. Ruoff, *Wordsworth and Coleridge: The Making of the Major Lyrics, 1802–1804* (New Brunswick, N.J.: Rutgers University Press, 1989); and Lucy Newlyn, *Reading, Writing, and Romanticism: The Anxiety of Reception* (Oxford: Oxford University Press, 2000). These three books follow an alternative path to a discussion of the clash of discourses, whose advantage is that it reconstructs a historical nexus or debate that has more claim to have existed before the critic described it—a debate explicitly written into the texts of poems.

19. Don H. Bialostosky, *Making Tales: The Poetics of Wordsworth's Narrative Experi-*

ments (Chicago: University of Chicago Press, 1984); And Don H. Bialostosky, *Words-worth, Dialogics, and the Practice of Criticism* (Cambridge: Cambridge University Press, 1992). I reviewed the second of these books in *Studies in Romanticism* 32, no. 2 (Summer 1993): 311–17. The point about Bialostosky's rhythmic telling, as a denial of telling rhythm, comes from a letter to me from Richard D. Cureton. Lynn Pearce is another in the small group of scholars of Romanticism who employ Bakhtin's terms not opportunistically but consistently: see her article, "John Clare's 'Child Harold': A Polyphonic Reading," in *Criticism* 31, no. 2 (Spring 1989): 39–57.

20. To descend from discourses to authors: the women poets were enormously popular in their moment—far more than Wordsworth and Coleridge; and the women made money from their works. Often they needed the money; they wrote to survive, most of them. Women poets were not avant-garde, in the sense of inventing new topics, new meters, new kinds of experience, or writing manifestos. But the male poets were consciously avant-garde, concerned for their own priority in discoveries. The male poets were among the group that started the possibility of an avant-garde in modern literature. Might this be one reason the males became the cynosure of critical attention for so long? Whatever the reason, the presence of the women poets complicates the table of discourses, disturbing the very idea of a period, if so many different things are going on in parallel in the same segment of time. When the women outflank the men on the progressive side of nearly all topics but literary innovation, it shows the male literary discoverers of the first Romantic generation as messy and irresolute in their relation to larger social movements. (See note 3, above. If second generation male poets are brought in, these male-female contrasts cannot be maintained. However, the second generation male poets were very likely influenced by the women poets of 1789–1815, as well as by Wordsworth and Coleridge.)

21. Josephine Miles, *Wordsworth and the Vocabulary of Emotion* (1942; New York: Octagon Books, 1965).

22. *The Prelude 1799, 1805, 1850,* ed. Jonathan Wordsworth, M. H. Abrams, and Stephen Gill (New York: W. W. Norton & Company, 1979). The 1805 edition is substantially the same as the 1850 but looser in sentencing and punctuation, so I use the 1850. Even here, almost fifteen years after the slavery question became a moral issue for him, Wordsworth cannot do what the women poets do forthrightly and consistently: condemn England as obviously inconsistent with its professed Christian beliefs, in its official position on the slave trade.

23. Amelia Opie, "The Negro Boy's Tale," from *Poems* (1802), quoted from *Romantic Women Poets: An Anthology,* edited by Duncan Wu (Oxford: Blackwell, 1998), 353–58. In his headnote to Opie, Wu states that the 1802 volume was popular and well reviewed, and that this poem was singled out by reviewers, for praise; however, the reviewer in *Edinburgh Review* made a dissenting remark that might require reply from readers of this book: "[Zambo's] argument on the natural equality of the Negro, and his sarcasms against those who practice not what they preach, are more in the character of the poet than of the supposed speaker" (quoted on 348).

24. In order of publication, here are three examples of the Romantic-Postmodern connection—the latter two each contain several contributions: Ira Livingston, *Arrow of Chaos: Romanticism and PostModernity* (Minneapolis: University of Minnesota Press, 1997); Edward Larrissy, ed., *Romanticism and PostModernism* (Cambridge, U.K.: Cambridge University Press, 1999); Martin Travers, ed., *European Literature from Romanticism to PostModernism* (London: Continuum, 2001).

25. Since the idea of textual voice is the main discriminator between the two poets to be compared here, let me expand on Bakhtin's relation to this category. This permits me to make a step outside his vocabulary.

In the 1920s, before the lid was screwed down on imaginative writing by Social Realist policies, Bakhtin knew and admired the work of the most extreme literary experimenters, Velemir Khlebnikov in poetry and Konstantin Vaganov in fiction. He does little more than mention these writers, however, and in his preferences for examples in his major work, he rarely gets closer to the twentieth century than Dostoevsky. And when he considers ancient, early Renaissance, and nineteenth century novels what he finds is the unity of person-idea, the unity of person-utterance. At the heart of his work, I have suggested, is a firm belief in utterance as emanating from an embodied moral person: the person-idea, not one without the other. Utterances emanate from persons, but also utterances cross between persons, social classes and nations. Starting when speech starts, the co-creators, alternating as speaker and addressee, fight out their differences on the territory of the utterance. That territory is the moving border between persons no matter how near or far they may be one to another in space/time.

Of course, a considerable sector of twentieth-century modern and postmodern literary work takes, as one main mission, the prizing apart of utterance and person. This is only the first step in a plan to deny, or put a partition between these very categories of person and utterance. This is apparently one way for writers to write themselves out from the influence and limitations of Romanticism. This is a valid enterprise, and superior works have resulted from such a program. I am thinking, to stay with Irish and British examples, of the brilliant questioning of authorial person in Samuel Beckett's "Texts for Nothing," or of the brutal uncanny clash of discourses of science and sociology and feeling in the poems of Jeremy H. Prynne, and of the non-sentence writings in animal-like sounds by Maggie O'Sullivan. At the end of chapter 1, I stopped my surveys of examples well before 1945 because I did not want to confront plural or vanished speakers with a Bakhtinian theory of utterance that cannot permit their existence.

This non-recognition of a major development of our era is one of Bakhtin's more serious limitations, from the point of view of poetry. Possibly the non-recognition can be turned to the advantage of his system; that is, a rescue might be possible, if one wants to argue that Bakhtin's dialogism is the essential critique *avant la lettre* of the politics and poetics of the anti-person avant-garde—even without his intending it.

26. Cary Nelson, ed., *Anthology of Modern American Poetry* (New York: Oxford University Press, 2000).

27. All references to these editions: Robert Pinsky, *Jersey Rain* (New York: Farrar, Straus and Giroux, 2000) (twenty-six poems in meter and mostly in rhymed stanzas); Charles Bernstein, *With Strings* (Chicago: University of Chicago Press, 2001) (sixty-nine poems mostly in free verse, though several poems are rhymed or partly rhymed—more often than not to mock the voice that would rhyme, yet also to show that for this writer rhyming is entirely possible). Because this is a study of discourses and not of single poems or poets, and due to delays on previous books when requesting and paying permission from living writers, I have adopted here a scheme of minimal quotation, so as to come just under the severe restrictions for "fair use" quotation. Readers who wish to check my analysis against the whole poems and books have here the full citation.

Bibliography

Bakhtin, Mikhail M. *The Dialogic Imagination: Four Essays by M. M. Bakhtin.* Ed. Michael Holquist, trans. Caryl Emerson and Michael Holquist. Austin: University of Texas Press, 1981.

———. *Problems of Dostoevsky's Poetics.* Ed. and trans. Caryl Emerson. Introduction by Wayne C. Booth. Minneapolis: University of Minnesota Press, 1984.

———. *Speech Genres and Other Late Essays.* Ed. Caryl Emerson and Michael Holquist, trans. Vern W. McGee. Austin: University of Texas Press, 1986.

———. *Art and Answerability: Early Philosophical Essays by M. M. Bakhtin.* Ed. Michael Holquist and Vadim Liapunov, trans. Vadim Limapunov and Kenneth Brostrom. Austin: University of Texas Press, 1990.

———. *Toward a Philosophy of the Act.* Trans. and notes by Vadim Liapunov, ed. Vadim Liapunov and Michael Holquist. Austin: University of Texas Press, 1993.

Batstone, Will. "Catullus and Bakhtin: The Problem of a Dialogic Lyric." In *Bakhtin and the Classics.* Ed. R. Bracht Branham. Evanston, Ill.: Northwestern University Press, 2001.

Bialostosky, Don H. *Wordsworth, Dialogics, and the Practice of Criticism.* Cambridge: Cambridge University Press, 1992.

Brandist, Craig. "On the Philosophical Sources of Bakhtinian theory of Dialogue and the Utterance." In *Bakhtin & His Intellectual Ambience.* Ed. Boguslaw Zylko. Gdansk: Wydawnictwo Uniwersytetu Gdanskiego, 2002.

———, and Galin Tihanov, eds. *Materializing Bakhtin: The Bakhtin Circle and Social Theory.* Houndmills, Basingstoke, Hampshire: Macmillan Press Ltd., 2000.

Ciepiela, Catherine. "Taking Monologism Seriously: Bakhtin and Tsvetaeva's 'The Pied Piper.'" *Slavic Review* 53, no. 4 (Winter 1994).

Coates, Ruth. *Christianity in Bakhtin: God and the Exiled Author.* Cambridge: Cambridge University Press, 1998.

Crawford, Robert. *Identifying Poets: Self and Territory in Twentieth-Century Poetry.* Edinburgh: Edinburgh University Press, 1993.

Cureton, Richard. *Rhythmic Phrasing in English Verse.* London: Longman, 1992.

Davidson, Michael. "Discourse in Poetry: Bakhtin and Extensions of the Dialogical." In *Code of Signals: Recent Writings in Poetics* (*Io* no. 30). Ed. Michael Palmer. Berkeley, California: North Atlantic Books, 1983.

Dentith, Simon, ed. *Bakhtinian Thought: An Introductory Reader.* London: Routledge, 1995.

Emerson, Caryl. "The Outer Word and Inner Speech: Bakhtin, Vygotsky, and the Internalization of Language." In *Bakhtin: Essays and Dialogues on His Work.* Ed. Gary Saul Morson. Chicago: University of Chicago Press, 1986.

———. "Prosaics and the Problem of Form." *Slavic and East European Journal* 41, no. 1 (1997).

———. *The First Hundred Years of Mikhail Bakhtin.* Princeton, N.J.: Princeton University Press, 1997.

———. "Bakhtin, Lotman, Vygotsky, and Lydia Ginzburg on Types of Selves: A Tribute," in *Self and Story in Russian History.* Ed. Laura Engelstein and Stephanie Sandler. Ithaca: Cornell University Press, 2000.

Erdinast-Vulcan, Daphna. *The Strange Short Fiction of Joseph Conrad: Writing, Culture, and Subjectivity.* Oxford: Oxford University Press, 1999.

Eskin, Michael. "Bakhtin on Poetry." *Poetics Today* 21, no. 2. Porter Institute for Poetics and Semiotics. Summer 2000.

Felch, Susan M., and Paul Contino. *Bakhtin and Religion: A Feeling for Faith.* Evanston, Ill.: Northwestern University Press, 2001.

Gardiner, Michael. *The Dialogics of Critique: M. M. Bakhtin and the Theory of Ideology.* London: Routledge, 1992.

Hirschkop, Ken, and David Shepherd, eds. *Bakhtin and Cultural Theory.* Revised and Expanded Second Edition. Manchester: Manchester University Press, 2001 (First Edition 1989).

———. *Mikhail Bakhtin: An Aesthetic for Democracy.* Oxford: Oxford University Press, 1999.

Hitchcock, Peter, ed. *Bakhtin/"Bakhtin": Studies in the Archive and Beyond.* Special Issue of *The South Atlantic Quarterly.* 97, nos. 3–4. Summer/Fall 1998.

Medvedev, P. N. *The Formal Method in Literary Scholarship: A Critical Introduction to Sociological Poetics.* Trans. Albert J. Werhle. Cambridge: Harvard University Press, 1985.

Meschonnic, Henri. *Critique du rythme: anthropologie historique du langage.* Paris: Edition Verdier, 1982.

Mihailovic, Alexandar. *Corporeal Words: Mikhail Bakhtin's Theology of Discourse.* Evanston, Ill.: Northwestern University Press, 1997.

Morson, Gary Saul, and Caryl Emerson. *Mikhail Bakhtin: Creation of a Prosaics.* Stanford: Stanford University Press, 1990.

Pearce, Lynn. "John Clare's 'Childe Harold': A Polyphonic Reading." *Criticism* 31, no. 2. Spring 1989.

Pechey, Graham. "Not the Novel: Bakhtin, Poetry, Truth, God." In *Bakhtin and Cultural Theory.* Ed. Ken Hirschkop and David Shepherd. Second Edition. Manchester and New York: Manchester University Press, 2001.

———. "Philosophy and Theology in 'Aesthetic Activity.'" In Susan M. Felch and Paul J. Contino, *Bakhtin and Religion: A Feeling for Faith.* Evanston, Ill.: Northwestern University Press, 2001.

———. "Intercultural, Intercreatural: Bakhtin and the Uniqueness of 'Literary Seeing.'" In *Bakhtin & His Intellectual Ambience.* Ed. Boguslaw Zylko. Gdansk: Wydawnictwo Uniwersytetu Gdanskiego, 2002.

Polan, Dana. "Bakhtin, Benjamin, Sartre: Toward a Typology of the Intellectual Cultural Critic." In *Discontinuous Discourses in Modern Russian Literature.* Ed. Catriona Kelly, Michael Makin, and David Shepherd. Basingstoke: Macmillan, 1989.

Rajan, Tilottama. "Romanticism and the Death of Lyric Consciousness." In *Lyric*

Poetry: Beyond New Criticism. Ed. Chaviva Hosek and Patricia Parker. Ithaca: Cornell University Press, 1985.

———. *The Supplement of Reading: Figures of Understanding in Romantic Theory and Practice.* Ithaca: Cornell University Press, 1990.

Renfrew, Alastair. "Them and Us? Representations of Speech in Contemporary Scottish Fiction." In *Exploiting Bakhtin.* Ed. Alastair Renfrew. Strathclyde Modern Language Studies, New Series, No. 2. Glasgow: University of Strathclyde, 1997.

Richter, David H. "Dialogism and Poetry." *Studies in the Literary Imagination.* Spring 1990.

San Diego Bakhtin Circle (Barry A. Brown, Christopher Conway, Rhett Gambol, Susan Kalter, Laura E. Ruberto, Tomás F. Taraborrelli, and Donald Wesling), eds. *Bakhtin and the Nation.* Special Issue of *The Bucknell Review* (43, no. 2). Lewisburg, Pa: Bucknell University Press, 2000.

Scanlon, Mara. "'In the Mouths of the Tribe': *Omeros* and the Heteroglossic Nation." In *Bakhtin and the Nation.* Ed. San Diego Bakhtin Circle. Lewisburg, Pa: Bucknell University Press, 2000.

Shakhinovsky, Lynn J. "Hidden Listeners: Dialogism in the Poetry of Emily Dickinson." *Discours Social/Social Discourse* 3, nos. 1–2. Spring-Summer 1990.

Shepherd, David. "Bakhtin and the Reader." In *Bakhtin and Cultural Theory,* Second Edition. Ed. Ken Hirschkop and David Shepherd. Manchester: Manchester University Press, 2001.

Sini, Stefania. "Intonation, Tone, and Accent in Mikhail Bakhtin's Thought." *Recherches Sémiotique/Semiotic Inquiry* 18, nos. 1–2. Montréal: Canadian Semiotic Association, 1998.

Thornton, William H. *Cultural Prosaics: The Second Postmodern Turn.* With a Preface by Donald Wesling. Edmonton: Research Institute for Comparative Literature, University of Alberta, Canada: 1998.

Tihanov, Galin. *The Master and the Slave: Lukács, Bakhtin, and the Ideas of Their Time.* Oxford: Oxford University Press, 2000.

Voloshinov, V. N. *Marxism and the Philosophy of Language.* Trans. Ladislav Matejka and I. R. Titunik. New York: Seminar, 1973.

———. "Discourse in Life and Discourse in Poetry" (1926). Trans. John Richmond. In *Bakhtin School Papers.* Ed. Ann Shukman. Russian Poetics in Translation, No. 10. Oxford: RPT Publications, 1983.

Wesling, Donald. "The Speaking Subject in Russian Poetry and Poetics Since 1917." *New Literary History* 23, no. 1. Winter 1992.

———. With co-author Tadeusz Slawek. *Literary Voice: The Calling of Jonah.* Albany, New York: State University of New York Press, 1995.

———. *The Scissors of Meter: Grammetrics and Reading.* Ann Arbor, Michigan: University of Michigan Press, 1996.

Zavialoff, Nicholas. "L'Énunciation chez Bakhtine: Un explication restrictive." In *L'Heritage de Mikhail Bakhtine.* Ed. Catherine Depretto. Bordeaux: Presses Universitaires de Bordeaux, 1997.

Zylko, Boguslaw, ed. *Bakhtin and His Intellectual Ambience.* Gdansk: Wydawnictwo Uniwersytetu Gdanskiego, 2002.

———. *Mikhail Bachtin.* Gdansk: Wydawnictwo Uniwersytetu Gdanskiego, 1994.

Index